THE GUILTY PARENTS
—SCREEN KIDS

A REASSURING GUIDE TO PARENTING SCREEN TIME,
PREVENTING DIGITAL ADDICTION, AND THE USES
OF TECHNOLOGY FOR POSITIVE CHILD
DEVELOPMENT

JOHN AND KIMBERLEY WOODS

CONTENTS

INTRODUCTION

"It's a beautiful day in the neighborhood." When Fred Rogers declared these words on September 21st, 1968, he changed the landscape of the content our children watched on television forever. However, even then, with a show most of us would now see as harmless, many parents fought against the "evils" of television.

Once *Mister Rogers' Neighborhood* began to speak to children on their level, but not in a condescending tone, the structure of kid's entertainment shifted. The shows viewpoint on ethics, children's emotions, and social conscience was revolutionary in its thinking. For parents who had feared their child's brains were rotting in front of the "idiot box," it was a massive stress reliever to know that the program they were watching was not only educational but taught them how to handle the stresses that would await them in later life.

Even though the wonderful world of Mister Rogers finished airing in 2001, all 895 episodes can still be streamed into homes all over the world by the wonders of the internet. I wonder how we would feel if our child was engrossed in an episode of such a classic show, over say, a mundane video of some YouTuber filming themselves while playing a video game, perhaps a little happier?

Now, how would we feel if, instead of our child watching good old Mister Rogers on the living room television, they were watching a streamed version on a tablet? A little different, I suspect. Maybe not a whole lot, but there is a definite stigma attached to tablets and phones—the same one that used to be reserved for television.

Screen time as a whole has a nasty stigma attached to it. The parents you know that may scoff when they are told how long your kids spend on their console or tablet almost certainly allow their own children to do the same. There is this odd unspoken acceptance that everyone is doing it but no one is talking about it. The key to finding a middle ground is allowing yourself to understand that technology is now a part of life.

We all worry when we see our children staring at a screen—it is one of the curses of being a good parent. Unfortunately, constant fretting and a belief that the decisions we are making may be detrimental to their development are something that we have to learn to live with (chances are not as detrimental as you may think). Yet, that is not to say that we cannot do things to ease our minds a little. Knowing the positives, as well as the negatives, of an issue that is so passionately disputed by our friends and social media can help us to take a more relaxed view on something that, in truth, can be used as a very effective tool in helping our kids to grow.

We understand that constant screen time can have an adverse effect on how our children develop, but the same can be said of almost anything that is consumed in unnatural amounts. When we lay out the facts to examine them and learn to regulate the time and content of the technology that our children ingest, we can at least rest a bit easier in knowing that a little time each day on their Xbox won't cause them to suddenly grow horns or have to be strapped to a bed while the digital demon that has possessed them gets eradicated by holy water.

What we aim to achieve in this book is to give you a bit more of a sense of calm the next time your kid asks if they can "go online" or point at your phone with puppy dog eyes. By giving some facts and advice in a laid-back, casual, and funny way (with plenty of research along the journey), we hope that your view on some of the horror stories attached to screen time will become a little less scary. Sometimes things get blown way out of proportion now-a-days.

However, first things first: I believe some introductions are in order. We are John and Kimberley Woods, and we are childhood sweethearts who have been together for over 24 blissful years.

John has multiple degrees in the field of Cultural Anthropology, Philosophy, and Physical Geography and has always had a passion for where we come from, how we think, and the world we live in.

Kimberley's background includes over 15 years of working with the public, with a big focus on animal care and rescue. She is also a wife, mother, and homemaker, which gives her the inside scoop when it comes to screen time and the effects of it.

Much like many of you who are reading this book, we have spent an endless amount of time discussing these very matters with our huge extended families, as well as our friends, colleagues, and neighbors. Conversations concerning screen time, and our children's usage of it, inevitably come up. Kimberley's heavy study of child development over the past four years and John's interest in tech development and how it affects people of all ages, all over the world, have helped us to fine-tune our opinions on the matter of technology and screen time as a whole.

In writing this book, we hope that our passion for parenting and understanding the stresses it brings will shine through. The negative information out there needs to be debunked, and we have a knowledge and passion about sharing these things as we know that we can help.

The benefits of what you will read will not only help your child in improving the content of what they watch, but it will also help you in becoming a bit happier and more fulfilled in your homelife. Screen time is one of the main causes of arguments in many households today, and if we can eliminate the negativity attached, then we can let some of the arguments fall by the wayside.

Throughout the book, we will cover such issues as video game violence; fears of laziness on both the parent and kids' side; passive and active screen time; using screens as a tool; bonding over screens; and much, much more.

You will learn to embrace many aspects of technology in your child's life and begin to understand that much of the information that is out there is extremely fear-biased. That is not to say that we will encourage you just letting your child become one with their PlayStation, far from it, but we will try to point you in the direction of the positives that sometimes get drowned in the sea of, often unfounded, negatives.

Tablets, phones, and consoles are all an inescapable part of life, and if we learn to accept this as fact, then we can start to figure out how we are going to integrate them into our lives to the point where we are not pulling our hair out at the sound of them being fired up.

In Sarah DeWitt's fantastic TED Talk, she alludes to these fears but lets us know that they can be harnessed in a positive way.

She opens by informing us that over 40% of American's check their phone within five minutes of waking and will continue to check it a minimum of 50 more times throughout each day (DeWitt, 2017).

What is interesting is when she tells us that we, as adults, consider our phones to be a necessity. We believe that our life would not function right without one. How could we not check it, when that parcel from Amazon is on the way? How will we know when it is two days away from delivery if we cannot check our phone?

This device, which we believe to be such an important tool, is exactly the thing that we want our kids to steer clear of. Surely, they are learning an important life skill by figuring out how to navigate it in a productive and positive manner? This is where teaching them about active screen time comes in, and we will discuss this more in-depth later.

However, the general rule still applies. If there is something in our lives that we consider to be vital, then we must raise our kids around it and guide them as best we can. This is how we, as parents, handle every obstacle that our children face as they grow. All we can do is teach them the things we know and hope that they make the correct choices in life. There will be tears of course, and conflict, but these are only little roadblocks that we have to learn to navigate around. And hey, if they are well-versed in phone usage, they can always pull up the GPS for us!

When we look at our kids engrossed in a phone or a tablet, it is very easy for us to let our minds drift to all of the terrible things that we have heard concerning the effects that they have on them. The cries of our nosey friend or interfering stranger can be muffled when we are decisive in our own decisions on what we are going to allow and what we are going to put our foot down about. When the chips are down, these are our kids, and as much as we will make mistakes along the way, we really do know what's best, so we need to believe that the information we are given concerning our fears for them is processed in the right way.

Picking up a book such as this one is a step in the right direction, as it means that you have pinpointed a problem, and you want to strive to do something about it. When we begin to build up our tools in the face of any adversity, not just about the pesky screen, we instantly step out of the realm of "worried," and into the position of "proactive."

Parenting is a skill that is constantly being improved as we go along, and most of the tips and tricks that we acquire have been seen or heard by us throughout our lives. The rest of them we learn by doing, and introducing some literature on the issues that have us on the fence will only help in figuring out which direction we want to step. However, we have to be careful where we tread, as there are a lot of things to step in if we listen to the wrong people as we walk. This, much like technology in our children's lives, is an unfortunate guarantee, and we will go into other people's negative influences in more detail in the "Opinions Are Like . . ." section.

Other chapters, like "Are Screens Turning My Child into a Criminal?" will delve into the always hot issue of video game violence and all of the negative press that goes along with it. Although these topics can be quite taboo, it is fundamental to discuss them and to put an end to a lot of the fears and notions attached. Knowing your enemy, so to speak, is important in laying the foundations of your new and improved outlook on things.

There will be no demands or condescension here, only well-thought-out suggestions and information that will assist you in building your very own set of rules and regulations when it comes to your children's screen time. Many of them you may already know, and some will be new to you, but with the mound of misinformation that pollutes social media and other outlets, it is always nice to open our minds to information that wasn't triggered by an emoji.

Along with our point of view on these subjects, we will intersperse some other findings and articles by bringing them into the narrative here and there along the way. This is not intended to bog you down in any way but only to back up the opinion that screen time is not necessarily the evil that it is sometimes pertained to be. We will lean more on the positive information as we want to be reassuring, I think we all know the negative information pretty well by now and personally we do not want to pile more on top of you. So we will weigh up the opinions in an attempt to help you to form a slightly more informed one of your own, and if you have a little giggle along the way, then where is the harm in that?

Most of the issues that we discuss in this book will have one underlying theme at the root: "Parental Guilt." This is a real and serious problem. In the workaday world that we live in, and a general need for two-parent incomes, the chances of parental guilt slipping into our minds can be quite common. That belief that we aren't there enough or that we are not spending the appropriate amounts of "quality time" with our children can influence us in our decision to insist that they switch the screen off and spend some time with us.

Wanting to spend time with our children is natural, and if you are someone who sets aside specific activities to do with your family, then more power to you. If we have a moment of clarity and suddenly decide that what is going on around us is not suitable, and we allow a knee-jerk reaction to sour the very valid point that we are trying to get across then we have to recognize how that might be received by our kids.

An article by Dena Kouremetis (2017) fills us in on the aforementioned parental guilt. She points out the very old adage of hindsight being 20/20. Even if our children grew up to be president or starting quarterback for the Green Bay Packers, we would still see something in us that we could have done differently.

What she tries to do is ease our burden a little, by telling us that "most parents have regrets" in the decisions we make concerning our kids. What we must do is not let them consume us in a way that makes us unhappy. Unless we are allowing our child to rule the roost and decide how much technology they use and what content they are watching, then we are most likely doing just fine. Letting too much guilt in over something that makes us human will eat us alive and leave us of no use to anyone (Kouremetis, 2017).

What she suggests is using the mistakes—they are most probably only perceived mistakes—as a process of self-improvement. If our kiddo reacts in an angry way after a two-hour YouTube session that just got away from us, then we will be more vigilant the next time. When little Johnny comes out of his room, and we do not recognize him, then a bit of sun and some restrictions are needed in the future. When little Olivia is watching a show on her tablet that encourages her to dance, then leave her alone because even though she is getting the urge to move from a screen, she is still moving.

The minefield that is screen time is much more easily navigated with a map. Throughout this book, we will give you the directions that you need to find a way through as unscathed as possible, by not only shining a light on screen time as a tool but by putting your mind at ease in the knowledge that the amount of time that you are currently allowing is most likely the norm, and if it isn't, then we will show you how to approach the matter and what can be done about it.

1

AM I A BAD PARENT?

This generation of parents are unique, as they are the first in human history that will have to make a decision on how beneficial and how destructive screen time is. However, like the commercialism of television or Elvis Presley, the evils of tablets will be long forgotten in the years to come. They will become, and already are, an essential part of life. Even what some people consider to be basic career paths have a need for some form of computer skills. Sometimes, it can just be hard for us to accept this as the new norm.

Sidonie Matsner Gruenberg, a Director of the Child Study Association of America, in a 1931 interview, alluded to the panic from the parents of the day regarding the commercialization of the transistor radio, a new in-home device at the time. She remarks that parents felt "helpless" against this "invader of the home" as they could not monitor it 24/7 (Ortutay, 2018).

What was the biggest worry that these parents had regarding it? It would interfere with conversation, study, interaction, group games, and reading. Sound familiar?

These fears were aimed at a creation that was designed to carry information instantly to the listener. Much like the Internet. In the same AP News article that mentions the concerns of Gruenberg in the 30s, the author, Barbara Ortutay, points to this very fact. When the Internet exploded onto the scene in the early nineties, it was touted as the "information superhighway" that was going to make learning and study easier than it had ever been, by blasting any data or knowledge that we required directly into our homes (Ortutay, 2018). Yet, flash forward a few decades, and the very thing that had been presumed to connect us all completely is now considered the soul cause for a death in human interaction.

When these massive shifts in the technological world occur, the fears of parents the world over are often quite grounded. Sitting in front of a black and white TV—watching nothing but *Bonanza* for 15 hours a day—will have the same detrimental effect as scrolling through an iPhone for the same amount of time. It is just the same parental issues in a different time.

Finding a balance will help, and dismissing the claims of your friends is vital. When you read a post from another parent that you know on Facebook, disregard it. They are either sugarcoating the truth, or they may be too strict. Do not be ashamed that your kids spend some time on their tablets, just understand that it is now an elemental part of life.

The days of endless knocks on the front door as the neighborhood kids line up outside with a baseball glove on their hands have faded. These things, like so much else now, are organized events in local parks and are attended by the parents. Hearing that *ping* on your child's phone is the new doorbell. Just because it is different from when we were kids doesn't make it bad. Try and imagine if Snapchat and Instagram had been as easily accessible in your youth. Would you have dismissed it or embraced it?

As parents, we are programmed to worry. It is what makes us who we are. This again is a good thing. The old adage of, "You will thank me when you're older" will always be a theme, and they will be grateful, even if it doesn't seem that way. Being able to give a satisfied nod of understanding when your grandchildren utter the same mumbled response that you once received from their parents, as they bury their head in technology, will be the gratification you need to prove that you did just fine.

However, you shouldn't have to wait until then. While we understand that communication through instant typed messages and a headset during a game of *Fortnite* are a part of life, we can start to give ourselves a bit of a break. Depriving your child completely of these things will only result in alienating them and causing unnecessary heartache for everyone.

Of course, teaching our children that life is not dependent on gratification from Facebook "likes" and Instagram "followers" is very important. I am sure we have all had our children tell us that they want to be a YouTuber when they grow up and cringed inwardly at this near impossible dream. Yet, didn't we all have similar expectations when we were kids? Only, we wanted to be an actor, or a musician, or a professional athlete. Not many kids will tell you that their dream is to be an office manager.

Endless screen time is another matter. When a child begins to immerse themselves in nothing but online interaction and the rapid-fire advertisements that inevitably accompany them, they can begin to lose touch with reality a little. This is where more stringent rules should be applied and the dreaded, "You will thank me when you're older" mantra must be uttered again. Do not fret. This is not your fault because, as we know, all kids are different. How many of us have one kid who wants nothing more than to play outside, while another seems to be constantly on the computer? We raised the two of them the same way, didn't we?

Educational games such as *Wordscapes* are available in abundance and games like Words with Friends that pit you up against other people exist too. Give your child a pencil and a Sudoku book, and they will look at you like you have three heads. Pull up a tab on a screen that has a Sudoku game on it, and they will smile and hug you. Both of them will challenge your kid in an equally productive way. The only difference is that if our friend walked in and saw them with the paper version, we would be proud. The screen? Ashamed. This is where changing our thinking comes into play because trust me, the person who walked through your door with their empty-handed kids in toe left their screens in the car.

It is hard for us to grasp that screen time is now a part of life. If your child has a love of books over tablets, then great. Yet, try and remember that before iPads and Xbox, not every kid picked up a book either. In truth, it was frowned upon in the school-yard as much as not having a tablet is now. Accepting that technology is now a fundamental part of life is not really a choice anymore—it is a fact. As we have already discussed, finding a balance of what they play and watch is where we come in.

Our children stumbling upon something that they shouldn't be watching on the Internet is a real and serious worry. It can be almost debilitating to us to imagine the horrors of what they may find. This is an issue for everyone, and you are well within your rights to lose a little sleep over it—we all do—but for the moment, it is quite unavoidable. Putting blocks and security on our WiFi will help a little, but at the end of the day, one of your children's friends will show them something that they found on their phone on the walk home from school. It is the modern-day "Wanna see a dead body?" issue. Kids are curious by nature, and all we can really do is teach them right from wrong and hope that they listen.

Everything that we watch on TV now is pre-recorded. The days of a watershed are gone, and the opportunity for them to click into something with violence and sex scenes is ever-present. Accepting that they will see and hear these things that were so taboo in our youth can help you to be prepared for explaining it to them when it happens.

Remember that you are not alone in this. Every parent, regardless of the front that they portray on social media, is going through the same thing. Just try not to be too hard on yourself when the kids power up the tablet.

OPINIONS ARE LIKE . . .

"Little Johnny only spends an hour a day on the Xbox," and "Olivia doesn't even own a tablet" are common phrases that will be shoved down our throats on a daily basis. Even if what the person is telling you is true, that is their business, and who is to say that what they are doing is right? Being a parent is as much about taking our hands off the wheel sometimes as it is about steering the car in the direction that we believe it should be going.

Every parent on the planet, since the beginning of time, is learning each day, and every generation has some new "evil" that they must protect their kids from. Heck even the Waltz was deemed for "prostitutes and adulteresses" when it first hit England in 1816, and there are similar stories with the Tango and the Charleston all the way up to modern dance moves like twerking.

When our grandparents played a record in reverse or danced the Funky Chicken at the town hall, they didn't instantly burst into flames as they did so. Yet, this was a common fear. Parents were told that these things would poison their children and lead them down a bad path. Technology is much the same. As with anything, it is only when it is consumed in excess that it really becomes a problem.

Other people's opinions mean nothing, and we should view them this way. This is a lot easier said than done, we know, but at least giving yourself a bit of a break from their words can help you to relax a little and even offer up some enjoyment watching your child play their games. Much like sitting around to play a board game together, partaking in your kids' screen time, even if we are only half-watching, is still time spent with them. And hey, they are a lot less likely to flip an Xbox over and storm off if someone else buys Boardwalk before they do.

There are no perfect parents. That picture you see posted on Facebook of your sister's smiling family took an hour to get everyone in place as screams and shouts raged all around them. Kids are kids, in any walk of life, and that means that they will be uncooperative and ungrateful at times. It is a natural part of life. Try not to be too hard on yourself when you are having a day where absolutely nothing goes to plan. Just concentrate on the things that went well.

Social media is saturated with opinions. It is the foundation of it, and the problem it causes is that most of the opinions are poisonous. It is far too easy for someone who is having a bad day to belittle another to make themselves feel a little better, and our parenting skills are usually the thing that we are most paranoid about. It is the one thing that we want to succeed at one hundred percent. Again, this is an impossibility and completely unattainable. Striving for perfection in something as unpredictable as raising a family will drive you into the ground. Try your best to ignore the opinions of others when you can.

This very thing is referred to in a 2020 article in Healthline, when we are advised to "spring clean" our "trusted circle" (Frost, 2020). By this, it means that toxic advice is just not needed. Remember to only discuss these issues with your partner—or anyone else who you can be sure that you not only trust—but know their reply will not make you feel like garbage.

The things that you beat yourself up about are happening in every home around the world. Know that when your child logs on to *Fortnite*, another 350 million kids are doing the same—and that is only at that one time. The number of kids logging in over a week is seemingly infinite. This is when depriving them of interacting with their friends is actually the real issue. Remember, this is their friends knocking at the door.

As we are aware of though, finding a balance is a tightrope walk that no one has, or ever will, perfect. The amount of time our kids spend on their screens will vary from day to day, and the importance of each time will be different for them, too. We need to remember that in school that day, several of their friends made plans to be online at a specific time, and when we disregard this as frivolous, we are dismissing something that is of monumental importance to them in a flash. What we are basically saying is that interacting with their friends isn't important, unless they do it exactly as we did.

However, try not to be too hard on yourself either. This is new to everyone and the long-term effects cannot be fully understood. If it becomes an addiction, then of course it will be damaging in the long run, but that goes for anything in life, not just technology. Believe that you will instinctively know the cut-off point because whoever gives you their opinion on it, is giving you just that: their opinion. Yours is just as valid as anyone else's on the subject.

Scrolling through Facebook can be like a minefield of bad news. It can seem that every second post is some character making you feel like you have failed as a parent. Letting what good there is on social media in and blocking the bad can seem like it is a hopeless effort at times. If you can manage to let other people's opinions slide more often than not, then you will be on the right path to understanding that you are the wonderful parent that everyone else knows you to be.

EACH CHILD AND PARENT ARE DIFFERENT

Information on parenting and especially on screen time is everywhere, and more often than not, it is contradictory. This is because there is no one answer. Everyone is still learning, and the positives and negatives can get confused in the mix. It is impossible to place a single heading over a subject as vast as this because every parent and child differs in some way.

Some kids will instinctively know how much screen time that they should have, and some will just not be that into it. Some will use them as a connection to friends and others will need it as an escape, as face-to-face interaction is a struggle for them. This has always been the case, only before kids lost themselves in books, collections, or any number of things. When this occurs, then the problem goes deeper than the technology itself, and the heartbreaking effort of making them go outside or face their fears comes into play.

Forcing your child to do something that they don't want to do, especially something that upsets them, is one of the hardest things that any parent will ever have to do. However, a lot of the time, it is very important in their growth. Helping them to understand that what they are feeling doesn't make them any different will help a little in convincing them that the thing they fear might just be what they need to help them find a bit more happiness. It won't be easy, but the payoff will be massive.

We as parents are different, too. Our own upbringing will shape our view on the things that we perceive to be important in life. Maybe sports and outdoor activity are what we believe to be the essentials. Others may feel that these things put their children in needless danger. Whatever the case may be, each belief and option will have its very own benefits, and much like screen time, we can never fully know the results of these decisions until many years later.

Pointing your child in the right direction, as far as technology is concerned, can be a tricky thing to do. We cannot know what form of technology will take their fancy, and with an abundance of choice, the options can seem endless. Some kids like nothing more than making funny faces with a Snapchat filter, while others prefer the online interaction of a group battle in *Fortnite*. These are no different from a taste in music, and as every child varies, we must learn to educate them on the pitfalls of each. In the end, they will choose their own path, and we can only hope that we guided them as best we could. At the end of the day, when they have their own kids, they will surely tell us we did it all wrong anyway!

Believing that we are doing some irreparable damage to our child's mental well-being is a never-ending fear. From mass media hype to watercooler gossip, we are bombarded with endless horror stories of the twisted minds that screen time will create. The majority of the people that spout this nonsense have kids who are using technology just as much as everyone else's and only feel a need to verbalize something so it seems a little less scary.

As each child grows, they will bring new challenges and new joys. Much like parents varying in their beliefs on the appropriate amount of sport and study their kids should have, a child will develop their own opinion on life as they grow. This will inevitably lead to disagreements, either with the parents or their siblings, but we must learn to only give in when we know we can. A little give-and-take is important, and extra screen time as a reward for a good report card or housework can be vital in teaching them the benefits of hard work. It will also help in enforcing the point that how much technology they can have is the parents' choice.

In a Koren Miller article from 2019, she points out that 68% of parents with children under five feel guilty about their kids using technology, so try and remember that you are not alone. "Mom guilt" or "parent guilt" are serious issues. When we let undeserved feelings of guilt into our thought process, we begin to make decisions that we never normally would.

This guilt can come in many different forms but all concerning screens. Around 47% said it was the neglect of family members, while 29% claimed that they feared their kids were wasting time and not being productive. These are all issues and worries that every one of us faces when we are watching our child with a screen. However, in understanding that virtually every single parent in the world is going through the same thing, we can start to take some of the unwarranted pressure that we have placed on ourselves off.

If you have more than one child then you can be productive while the other one is online too. Allowing one child to be distracted while spending time with friends online can give you time to focus on your other kid or kids. Giving one on one time they may not often receive in a busy household with multiple siblings. Using screen time in this way may counter the feelings of family neglect as you can maximize your family time with another child and then flip this around the next day.

Thankfully for the world, Elvis Presley's music survived as have the various frowned upon dances throughout history. Even if we are not a fan of technology in our children's lives, we have to accept that it will be around for the long haul, too. What we need to do is embrace it, and learn to enjoy it with our children because it is a very important part of their lives and always will be. The world that they are growing into almost insists on it, and helping them to understand it as best they can will help them to enjoy the benefits and be mindful of the rest.

2

AM I A LAZY PARENT?

The short answer to this question is no. The long answer? No. Letting your children have a little screen time while you do the washing, or take an important work call, or make dinner, does not make you a lazy parent in any way. Hell, letting your child watch a YouTube video while you read a book or take a bath doesn't make you a lazy parent—it makes you human.

Screen time can be a useful tool when used correctly. We all want a happier home, and sometimes, if not always, that involves a calmer, more fulfilled parent. Remember that when you begin to look after yourself, the little things that bogged you down all day fade away, and the quality time that follows is far more enjoyable.

Taking time to ourselves is essential. When the weight of the world is weighing us down, even the smallest issues can become massive, and our reaction to them can be aggressive and over the top. This, of course, leads to tensions, and even though we feel bad for shouting, it can sometimes be hard to admit that we were wrong and let it go. Instead, we bottle it up and dig our heels in, which only creates more tension in the process.

This stems from us not allowing any time for ourselves. Self-love and "me time" are not ugly terms. We know the "perfect parents" that you see on your Facebook feed would have you believe as such, but wanting a little time to relax or go on a date night does not make you in any way lazy or selfish. It is fundamental to our well-being and growth. So, if you just have to know if Rachel really got on the plane in *Friends* for the 20th time, or if there's a playoff game on TV, then do not be afraid to just park their butts in the playroom and fire up the tablet every once in a while. Also, do not feel guilty in any way that you want that time for yourself, we can't just limit our adult time to the afterhours of our kids bedtime.

Time out of the house with your partner or your friends is needed too. We all love our kids to the point where it hurts, but if we spend 24/7 in their company, everything will begin to tick us off. This is not a reflection on you as a parent, it is just a fact of life that living in someone's company for an endless period of time will eventually begin to grate on you. How many times can your partner cut their toenails in front of you or tell you about the person at work that they hate before it makes you want to pull your teeth out? The same applies to our kids. As much as we want to be the all-calm, all-playful parent that our friends are (they're not really), it is an unattainable goal, and it will drive you into the ground in the end if you try and hold on to it.

A 2017 article by Bonnie Gibbs Vengrow points to the fact that 59% of parents believe that they spend enough quality time with their children, whereas more than half of parents claim that they do not get enough time away from their children to do "adult things." This is a need that can sometimes make us feel unnecessarily selfish, which is wrong.

She goes on to point out that "mom guilt" is a very real, and very detrimental issue. Letting yourself enjoy a little time to yourself or with your partner is actually good for your kids, as a more relaxed you will be a better parent (Vengrow, 2017).

Vengrow finishes by telling us that if a parent feels too overwhelmed with chores and general kid stuff, that we must "start small." She says to begin with giving yourself five minutes unaccompanied. Just long enough to "sit and look out the window," or just lie down alone and think of nothing. Once you begin to realize that everything didn't fall apart when you stepped away for a few minutes, then you can begin to take a little bit more each time, and before long, you won't feel that guilt for taking a yoga class or dinner with your loved one.

Organize a regular "date night," "guys night," "girls night," or just a Burger King and a podcast in the car for two hours while the babysitter earns their cash. However, make sure that whatever one you choose, you go through with it. A more relaxed you will be more fun to be around, and the screen time that you then allow will cease to eat away at your conscience.

This all applies to single parents too, we know it may seem harder to find the time, but you need to fall back on Nana and Grandpa when you can. Anyone who raises kids alone deserves all of the happiness the world can give to them. You are the true heroes in this world, yet you do not get half the credit that you deserve. If anyone has earned a night out on the town, or a spa day, it is you!

Single parents need to have their babysitter on speed dial. This again is not something to feel guilty about. You do not have the freedom of falling back on your partner when things get heavy, and you need to know that there is someone on the other end of the phone that can step in when little Johnny is trying your last nerve. If the babysitter is busy, then drop them off at a trusted friend's house—preferably one that won't scoff and roll their eyes when you do, as that is the last thing you need.

Don't be afraid to have other parents and their kids over to your place either. Leave the anxiety of an untidy house behind and invite them over, trust me no one will care. This is a great way for any parent to let off some steam. When there is a group of kids together, they basically entertain each other, which leaves more time for you to have some wine and snacks with the other exhausted folks. Social life does not end with having children— it only shifts a little.

Enjoying yourself will help you to be more relaxed around the home. The feeling of being left behind in our social life when we have kids is a real and serious thing. Studies have shown (we have to go there, sorry!) that depression and anxiety at the thought of being excluded after the birth of our children have increased dramatically with our growing dependence on social media. How often, when we are up to our eyes in laundry and Skype calls, have we seen some party or event that our single, childless friends are attending pop up on Instagram? It can hurt, and it can make us feel that the path we are on has become separated from the main road.

This is where finding time to go out with our friends and partners becomes essential. When that picture of Robyn doing a tequila shot or Mike smiling broadly while holding an enormous bowl of chicken wings appears on your feed, and you start to feel like your social life was a thing of the past, knowing that you have a night out planned on the weekend will take all of the sting out of it. Most of the time, the worry that claws at us, is only a fear that we have been forgotten about. We haven't: People had nights out without us long before we had kids, we just never paid it any attention.

Never presume that you are a lazy or selfish parent for wanting a bit of time to yourself. Making yourself happy is doing everyone else around you a favor, too.

PASSIVE VS. ACTIVE AND EDUCATIONAL SCREEN TIME

When we consider screen time, we can sometimes fall into the trap of believing it all to be negative. Often, the time our kids spend on their tablets or consoles can be broken down into two separate categories. Here, we will look at the benefits and dangers of each one.

Active and Educational Screen Time

This is the time spent on technology where the brain is activated in a good way. Educational games are very easily accessible, and many of them are structured in such a way that your child will have a lot of fun as they play.

There are plenty of apps on phones and tablets that involve nothing more than your kid drawing a picture or coloring in pre-existing pictures. Any game like this will involve creativity, and much like the Sudoku paradox that we discussed earlier, sometimes because it is on a screen, we tend to look at it negatively. If our kid was lying on the floor with crayons and paper, we would have no issue, but drawing on a tablet will have as much of a positive effect. And hey, there will be nothing to tidy up after.

Active screen time can be when your kid makes their own YouTube videos. These videos do not ever have to be posted online, but the process of creating them will be all your child is interested in, and the creativity and effort that it takes will be beneficial in an abundance of ways. Arts and crafts of all kinds will be needed for them to make their little show, and it is always something that we can be a part of, too. Watching your child create something from scratch that is wholly theirs is one of life's most beautiful moments.

Sometimes, all your kid wants to do is build a fort or lay out their toys in a creative way. These are the things that we have been hoping they would do. The only difference is that they want the phone on record as they do so. Where is the harm in that? Another plus to this is that while they are making their video, they are talking to the room and building up skills such as public speaking and communication as they go along. All of these things are positive.

Many spelling games exist, and the joy in your child's face as they reach a higher level or learn a new word will only be surpassed by yours as the pride kicks in. Of course, a saturation of educational games is still endless screen time, and this cannot be good. However, steering them in the direction of games and apps that spark their creativity will be good for them in moderation.

For older kids, getting them to write a blog (again, this never has to be posted) will open their mind up to the passion of creating with words. This is another one where we would be thrilled if they were scrawling away in a notebook, yet we feel bad when it is on a laptop. Letting your child produce something from nothing is a wonderful thing, and who knows what passions might be unleashed from the process? Once they see the joys and the creativity involved in writing, they may be naturally intrigued to pick up books and immerse themselves in something that they have learned to love.

Find some educational games that suit you and try to play some competitive word games with your kids. Encourage your kids to express themselves with the technology of today, who knows, maybe someday they will become a successful YouTuber or Social Media Influencer!

Passive Screen Time

This is where it can get a little tricky. Passive screen time is when your child watches some repetitive junk that triggers no real thought or effort. It usually occurs when YouTube or the like is on autoplay, and the watcher only has to sit back and let the next 15 minutes of rubbish consume them.

How many times can they watch some honey-voiced woman's hands unwrapping L.O.L. Surprise dolls before it becomes destructive? These videos do not really achieve anything but calmness in our child, but after a certain amount of time, it will only lead to binge-watching. Yet, much like guilty pleasures for us (Did Rachel get on the plane?), we must allow them some time to chill out—even if the voice from the tablet makes us want to run out into the street naked with a chip bag on our head.

For our older kids, passive screen time will involve endless scrolling through social media feeds. This is part of their lives now and it is a minefield of arguments when the subject is broached, but teaching them early that tablets and phones are not our lifeblood will hopefully help them to understand that talking to someone face-to-face far outweighs any video of a chicken wearing shoes.

Always remember, a lot of habits that our kids pick up when it comes to screen time, they get from us. Who here can honestly say that they haven't snapped out of it half an hour after opening Facebook on their phone and realized that absolutely no information went in? "Do as I say but not as I do" will always cause arguments, as the incredulous look that your child gives you is probably deserved.

There are always apps that you can purchase with "Kids" versions on them. Netflix, YouTube, and almost all streaming services will have these options. They are a great stress reliever and will give you peace of mind in knowing that they are watching child-friendly videos.

Microsoft, Apple, and PlayStation all have screen time limits that can be set. Just clicking on their websites can open up a whole new plethora of options and tools to help you keep a limit to your child's viewing. These things are there for a reason, so do not be afraid to use them.

As we briefly touched on in Chapter 1, your children will never be perfectly protected from hearing and seeing things that they shouldn't. It is unfortunately one of the prices we have to pay for living in the digital age. The best we can do is teach them that these things are wrong, and hope that they understand. We have to remember, though, that some of the things that would have shocked us as kids will have little or no effect on them. That is not to say that there aren't things out there that will scar them, as we all know that there is.

THE IPAD NANNY AND BACKGROUND TV

If you are paying good money for someone to watch your kids while you have your well-deserved night out, then they should not be just parking them in front of a screen and eating your food. The screen time (the guilty pleasure screen time) that you allow your kids is yours to give. You have earned it, as you have spent the rest of the week finding endless ways to entertain and educate them without it.

The flip side of this, of course, is when someone comes over to watch them for an hour as a favor while you go to the gym or take an important work call. These are the free pass times where you are just glad for the help and want to make it as easy as possible on the person who is lending a hand. Do not feel guilty about this. The last thing you want after you have spent an hour on yourself, or had a busy meeting, is to come home to your child upset and your friend pulling their hair out.

Babysitting is a skilled job, and if you are paying good money for a service, you should expect the best quality. It is not rude to leave a list of activities that you would like them to partake in. Taking the kids to the park or playing outside is the bare minimum that you should expect, and as we all know, our kids always seem to jump with joy when the babysitter or Grandma suggests doing something that they would have rolled their eyes at had we mentioned it.

An experiment on background TV, in which 50 children under the age of two were given toys to play with for an hour, showed some interesting results. For half of this hour, a television showing a game show was played in the background. During the half hour that the television was on, the kids would look up for a few seconds every minute or so, this may seem insignificant but their attention was still disconnected from play. Although they did not spend long looking at it, creativity, focus, and human interaction were acutely disrupted by something that was of no real interest to them (Schmidt et al., 2008).

This sort of early introduction to television and the escape that a screen can provide is almost impossible to avoid. At times, plonking our toddler in front of *Paw Patrol* is the only time that we get things done. The best that we can do is to be vigilant in how we control it as they grow.

As they progress to the point where they can use a tablet themselves, there will inevitably be times when arguments will ensue. All that our child knows is that we are keeping them from their "fix," and they want to know why. This is where active and educational screen time comes into play. We cannot just give in every time they get a bit heated, but we can steer them in the direction of positive games or videos.

Anger will be part of these interactions. It is hard for us to watch as someone we love wants to do something destructive, so take a breather, and do not react. Try to understand that screen time is part of their life, and all they want to do is watch a video that brings them joy, regardless of the fact they now know by heart which L.O.L. Surprise doll the lady unwraps next.

Allowing constant screen time is not an excuse to be an absent parent. This is just a fact. Knowing the difference between being actively involved in how much time they spend on their tablet or what game they are playing is massively different from shrugging your shoulders and saying, "What can you do?"

We must always be aware of the length of time that is being spent consuming technology, and we have to strive to steer them in the general direction of educational and active apps.

Remember, sometimes it is okay for them to watch that video which drives us mad, or to join in with their friends in *Fortnite*. It does not make you a lazy parent if you allow this from time to time. Gaming and social media are a part of their lives, and depriving them of it completely is akin to alienation from their social circles.

Hey, if they are busy for an hour and you fancy a hot bath or sometime to watch that game you recorded days ago, then where is the harm in that?

3

ARE SCREENS MAKING MY KID DUMB?

This has been a question that parents have been asking themselves ever since two rectangle bricks played tennis on a screen. Long before the sprawling worlds of *Black Ops* and *Fortnite*, parents have wondered if the time they are allowing their children to spend playing video games is doing long-term damage to them. Just like most things that are consumed in moderation, it is not.

Think of wine: When it is enjoyed in a minimalist fashion, like a glass of red with dinner, it is widely known to have a lot of health benefits. It is only when it makes the switch from enjoyment to a need that it becomes extremely detrimental to our health. Video games and the levels of consumption that we allow our kids are much the same.

Sometimes, as parents, we can become more focused on the *type* of game, more so than the time spent playing it. As hard as it is for us to understand when our child is blasting all of his friends to pieces on the screen in front of them, first-person shooters (FPS), and other games in the same category, are just a part of life now. The image of a grumpy teenager with dark makeup and a trench coat on, becoming angry at the world because of the violent video games that they are playing, is a myth. The issues that develop in kids that are this extreme are always caused by something a lot deeper.

Games have been known to increase the levels of dopamine that is released in the brain, which is proven to benefit focus, planning, and a peaked interest in other subjects. It is essential in our structure as human beings. And when it is triggered in the brain, it turns the amino acid (tyrosine) into dopamine.

Now, we do not want to get bogged down in a load of scientific terminology and jargon, but what it breaks down to is that increased dopamine has been proven to help with:

- Learning
- Sleep
- Heart rate
- Movement
- Dexterity
- Mood
- Attention

- And many more important benefits

Even something as serious as ADHD, which ironically is often used as a stick to beat screen time with, can be helped with controlled exposure to technology. It is not a miracle cure, of course, but the medication, Ritalin, works by releasing dopamine into the brain. This is the same dopamine that is naturally released when playing certain fast-paced games and FPS.

Increased dopamine release has also been proven to help in the long term with horrific diseases such as Parkinson's Disease, schizophrenia, depression, dementia, seasonal affective disorder, obesity and the previously mentioned ADHD, to name but a few.

In the case of obesity, the part of our brain that acts as our natural reward system can sometimes need a lot more food until we can feel fully satisfied. Increased dopamine can help reduce the amount that must be consumed in order for us to accept that we have had enough. However, as we have mentioned previously, plonking our child in front of a screen for the whole day will not suddenly make them healthy. Quite the opposite.

Moderation is the key. We must learn to understand how much time is healthy and how much is detrimental to our children. When we find a balance that benefits us both, then the day becomes a lot easier, as our children and ourselves will feel a lot more satisfied and fulfilled. Consistency with rules lowers the rate of arguments and remember, there are educational games out there too, if they really must play something.

The modern world is becoming more and more a technology-based one. Gone are the days when having computer skills lifted you above the crowd. Today, not having them is what stands out, and a young adult going out into the workforce for the first time will be threatened with being left behind if they cannot keep up with the ever-changing world of computers and everything that goes with them.

This applies to their social lives, too. Being up to date with the latest app or social media tool is a massive part of a young person's life now. It would not be very nice for them at a party when all of their friends are pulling up pictures on their phones of them posing in a "cat filter" while our child whips out a dusty polaroid photo of them with their grandma. Much like the must-have toy or Nintendo in our youth, keeping up with the trends in technology is of vital importance to the kids of today.

Young children will often learn their letters, numbers, shapes, and colors from YouTube videos, and as much as the aforementioned video of L.O.L. Surprise dolls being unwrapped can try our last nerve as we subconsciously mime the rotation they are doing for ourselves, the movement and colors will help with cognitive functions in the long run. It is just hard to see it when our brain unwillingly says, "Go-Go Girl is next" as we are making dinner.

Video chatting is a massive plus to come from the technology boom. Our young kids having the option to call Nana and Grandpa at the swipe of a finger is a wonderful thing, for both the child and our folks. That closeness is extremely important, and our children making the decision themselves will only lead to independence and the importance of human decency and caring. And who wouldn't like a spontaneous call from their kids or grandchildren?

Zoning out for hours on end in front of a screen is detrimental, as we all know. Dedicating massive portions of our day to seemingly frivolous things for that amount of time can never have a positive effect, but as we keep pointing out, it is the "quality versus quantity" aspect that we are trying to achieve. So, if you walk into the bedroom and your child hisses and melts a little when you switch on the light, then let's agree that they have had too much time online, and an exorcist should be called immediately.

In all seriousness though, when it is time to turn the screen off, then it is time to turn it off, and you must stand firm in your decision. If they don't like it, then that is just something they will have to deal with, and taking an authoritative stance early on and holding your ground is fundamental in your child's health. If they get upset, then just say, "You will thank me when you're older," for the 600th time.

SCREENS AS A TOOL

- *W*ordscapes
- Poptropica
- Fun Brain
- Mr. Nussbaum
- PBS Kids Games
- National Geographic Kids
- Academic Skill Builder
- BBC School Games
- Sheppard Software
- Curious George Math Game

These are just a grain of sand in the coastline of fun, educational games that are available for kids. Even *Minecraft* has positives to give, in that it teaches increased creativity, resource management, geometry, problem-solving, and teamwork. Hey, parents can play, too. Not all games are detrimental to our children's health, and the educational ones can be fun as well as positive.

There are thousands of games that provide little or no benefit, but like us, kids need some time when they partake in things that are for pleasure alone. Trying to teach them that everything they do should have a productive outcome will only lead to anxiety, and as they grow older, they will presume that taking joy in anything is wrong. At the end of the day, we want our children to be happy in life, and part of that is sometimes enjoying the things that we know are a little wrong.

A common belief is that your child is just going numb in front of a screen. This is untrue, and unless they are doing so for the majority of the day, then a little screen time is not going to hurt. In actuality, it can be beneficial. Only when it gets to the point where you have to toss broccoli into their mouth from a distance as they play, like a seal at feeding time, has it become a serious problem.

Daphne Bavelier, a Cognitive Psychologist, explains during one of her TED Talks, that first-person shooters can help with a variety of things, including dexterity, vision, problem-solving, and multitasking.

Of course, she goes on to point out that the benefits will only be achieved by using our screens in moderation. These are things that we already know, but concentrating a little more on the positive points that she raises can help us to build up more acceptance when our child is lost in an online game (Bavelier, 2012).

Another interesting point she makes is that the average age of a gamer is 33 in 2012. This can give us a little window into the fact that adults are making the exact same choices that our kids are making and still, for the most part, managing to live productive lives alongside their screen time. In fact, a 2021 article that pieced together multiple statistics found that 70% of gamers are

18 or older and the average gamer is 34 with a house and children. Knowing that it is now a part of life is something that we can use when figuring out how long our child should be online.

In a world where 90% of children play video games or use technology of some kind as a pastime, steering them in the direction of some of the educational games that we listed will help in their development for the world outside of the screen. Acquiring new knowledge is one of life's most rewarding pleasures, and the need to discuss it with someone that you love can be almost uncontrollable at times. This is the same for adults and children alike, and the moment when our child first explains something to you that you were not aware of is magical for both of us.

When our kids begin to use screens as a tool (the times when we can get them to), we can be a lot more proactive and in tune with how they are affecting them. Knowing that the games or apps that they are using are benefiting their progression in life is calming, and it will lead to a happier household, which is something that we all want.

As your child is learning to navigate a tablet and all the intricacies that come with it, they are preparing for a life that will inevitably be massively influenced by it. There is nothing that we can do about the shape of the world today, only accept that technological skills and know-how are a fundamental part of life. Apps and games may seem removed from using technology productively in later life, but the comfort and ease that they learn will all be part of the online life of instant responses and information that awaits them. Using the educational games as some of their screen time is essentially killing two birds with one stone, as the skills they acquire along the way will be important when the time comes.

Take *Wordscapes*: Although it is considered an adult game, the slow progression in the difficulty of the words you must find is quite achievable for a child who has only been reading for a few years. As your child completes the quick-fire levels each time, they will not only be learning, but they will find endless joy in having competed in a game aimed at their parents. When a child begins to view knowledge as a quest and a privilege, the thoughts of learning something new become a gift to them. Letting them into our world sometimes makes them feel important, and a need to be like their parents will, in turn, encourage them to push on in a game that is teaching them the whole time.

Unfortunately, much like the apple that has turned brown in the fruit bowl, upon hearing that some games are beneficial to them, your child might suddenly find the idea unappealing. A playful shake of the finger and a cross face as they fire up an educational game might help the process seem a little more fun to them. A bit of reverse psychology never hurt anyone.

VIDEO GAMES AND VIOLENCE

Watching on as our sweet little child blows street scum to smithereens on the screen before us can be unnerving; the joy it brings them can be frightening; and the ease at which they do it can be terrifying. However, fear not, as FPS are not the life-scarring games that they were first thought to be.

Many of them will have a "kids" setting to remove blood and carnage if that is what the game involves; games like *Fortnite* have no blood and gore at all. When we sit down and actually watch some of these games unfold, a lot of the time they are no more graphic than an episode of *Star Wars: The Clone Wars*. It is only when we hear the rapid-fire gunshots and our child's squeals of delight as he laughs through the headset with his pals do we begin to let the dreaded opinion of our friend, the "perfect mother," creep into our minds.

Fearing that our child will lose touch with reality if they play too many "violent" video games is expected, but the truth of the matter is that there have always been worries like this—long before Rockstar decided that dragging people out of their cars and stealing them was the basis for a multibillion-dollar franchise.

When our grandparents read comic books that depicted violence, their parents might have sat by the old black and white TV at night and discussed their mutual fear that little Johnny would grow up to be a murderer if he kept reading those silly things. Those same parents where likely the topic of discussion in their generation for listening to nonsensical radio shows.

Steering our children in the right direction and giving them the understanding of what is reality and what isn't is far more important than what games they play. Right from wrong has been the same, and furthermore, it will never change. Ethics are what we do when nobody is taking note, and only we as parents can pass these beliefs down to our children. When we start to blame society and technology for our child's perceived failings, then we are sailing into "lazy parent" territory, and we all know that this is not the case. If it was, then you wouldn't be reading something that is aimed at reinforcing your already strong parenting skills.

The carnage that is happening on the screen is no different from the video games that were played years ago. All that has changed is the visuals and the ability to play with multiple people around the globe at any one time. It is only when the violence on the screen is so expertly detailed that we really feel like what we are seeing just has to be damaging. However, crimes and violence in the real world have always been there, so if little Olivia shouts, "YES, HEADSHOT!" from her bedroom from time to time, try to understand that it doesn't mean that she will hide behind a grassy knoll one day. It's just her spending some time with her friends.

Criminals are made from a lot more than screen time. Surroundings and upbringing far outweigh anything that a few million pixels on a TV can do. Teaching our kids the basics of life from an early age will keep them from ever blurring the lines between what is happening on screen and what is acceptable in the world outside of the virtual one.

We must reinforce the point that when they are saturated with screen time, it will be devastating to them in the long run. Nobody, child or adult, can function successfully if all they have ever known is screens—it is just not possible. What we have to do as parents is draw a line in the sand and insist that the rules we have set down are obeyed. This does not have to be done aggressively, but if we lay the rules down early, and reward good behavior when necessary, then everything will naturally fall into place.

When ethics are instilled in their home life, then they carry over into every aspect of their life thereafter, and what they see on the screen from then on will be deciphered in their minds appropriately and broken down into what is real and what isn't. As we know, there will be times when they stumble upon something disturbing that is out of our control, but when they know that you are understanding of these things, they will surely then discuss it with you, and you can put their mind at ease.

FPS and racing games are proven to have a lot of benefits. This may sound like a cop-out, but letting ourselves accept that they do is important. Once we do, we can lay off it a little bit more when the time comes for our kids to have a little guilty pleasure and play a game that makes us slightly uncomfortable. Just set a time limit beforehand, and stay vigilant on the amount that is spent playing it.

The next time that you are worried about the games your child is playing turning them into a criminal, just know that Ted Bundy didn't have an Xbox.

4

IS SCREEN TIME MAKING MY KID LAZY?

One of the biggest worries for any parent is the fear that some of the decisions that we make will cause long term-effects for our children. Are they reading enough? Are they exercising enough? Are they eating healthy? Am I allowing them to become lazy?

The answer to all of these questions is no, but as we have discussed previously, it is only 'no' if you are not indulging their every whim and spoiling them with the amount of treats and freedoms that you allow. If your child eats nothing but sugary snacks because "They hate it when you say no," then they will be overweight and unhealthy. If they do not study enough, they will not be top of their class. If they spend six hours a day doing nothing but sit in one spot and stare at a screen, they will become lazy.

Many problems that parents face stem from falling into bad habits. This does not make you a bad parent if it happens—it only makes you human. If you are able to become aware that a standard has slipped and rectify it, then you and your child are on a positive path to success. It is only when we notice the bad habits that have become the norm and do nothing about it that things start to get messy.

Staying on top of our kids is never easy. Being "the bad guy" can not only be hard, but it can lead to arguments among the two parents as one will always feel that the other is getting a free ride by being the "fun" one. Even when your child turns out their bottom lip and stomps the ground with their foot, you must remain strong and stand by your convictions. Giving in will only lead to more bad habits, and the snowball effect will be devastating.

Screen time does not have to mean lazy time. There is an endless supply of physical games and apps out there that encourage movement and exercise. Most of them will be so sugarcoated that your child will have no idea that they are doing something positive for themselves. They range from toddler to young adult and are designed in such a way that movement and exercise become a part of life.

The Nintendo Wii, for example, consists solely of physical games that are mostly aimed at kids. Most games will involve punching, jumping, dancing, swinging, and of course, laughing, which will help in all sorts of ways and let your child know that exercising is not a punishment, but something that releases endorphins, and in turn, happiness and joy.

Most of the games on the Wii are family-oriented, so don't be afraid to join in with your children when they are playing. Watching their parents flail about like an upturned turtle is bound to cause shrieks of laughter and encourage them to try and beat the grown-up's score. Don't be afraid to make a fool of yourself for their entertainment. This is actually a good approach to take with your kids in general, as showing them that embarrassment is only a state of mind will strengthen them against shyness in the years that follow.

There is also an abundance of nature apps out there, and taking your kids for a walk on a beautiful summer day as they get notifications explaining all the wondrous things that they have passed on their walk will bring a lot of joy. These apps are aimed at enlightening your child in science and nature while also raising their exercise levels. The fresh air alone will be a plus.

Some of the apps that offer these great services are:

- Star Walk Kids
- Rainforest Day
- Meet the Insects: Forest Edition
- Audubon Owls
- World Atlas
- Nature Tap
- Geocaching

These wonderful apps will not only pique your child's interest in all of the nature around them, but they will also get their little legs moving and provide the type of bonding that lasts a lifetime. Being outdoors with our kids is a beautiful thing; the fresh air and the sense of togetherness is priceless and should be cherished. Plus, if they learn a little something along the way, then where's the harm in that?

Many TV shows such as *Yo Gabba Gabba!* and *The Wiggles* encourage movement. The dancing and exercise in them are shown in a fun, yet informative way, and the children who watch are kept moving throughout, preventing the dreaded stop and stare that always leads to zoning out. Most of these shows run throughout the morning on children's channels and are also easily accessible through Netflix and other major streaming sites.

There is a massive difference between games and endless scrolling. Games, as we know, are perfectly fine in moderation and are used as just a little bit of fun. Our children wanting to do something that makes them happy for an hour or two in the evening is perfectly natural, and we should always view it as such. It is only when it switches from a pastime to multimedia tasking that it becomes an issue.

We have all had those moments when we have tried to communicate with our child as they scroll through what basically boils down to nothing and only received a grunted answer. Sometimes, the thing that grates on us the most is the fact that we know we can be caught doing the same thing ourselves. At these times, it is best to steer them toward an educational or fitness-based game. Even though it is their allocated screen time, it doesn't mean that they should be allowed to become one with the couch as their thumb scrolls the screen repeatedly.

Screen time is only ever detrimental when our children become consumed by it. Fitness-based games and apps that encourage nature walks will help give our children the much-needed exercise that their body and mind need. The energy that is released from these activities will lead to happiness and fulfillment in both your child and yourself.

Remember, the next time the sight of one of your kids staring at a tablet like they are hypnotized stirs up anger in you, take a breath and switch on the Wii—don't be afraid to make a fool of yourself for their entertainment.

LEAD BY EXAMPLE

We have touched on this a little already, but leading by example is of vital importance. When our child sees us mindlessly scrolling through Facebook, or when an hour of looking at all of the beautiful people on Instagram has made us feel like a "before picture," understand that they will feel very aggrieved that you are doing the exact thing that you yelled at them for doing a few hours before—and rightly so.

It is very unfair of us to spout the words "Do as I say but not as I do" from our technological pedestal and not expect a reaction. Unfortunately, even with all of our knowledge and know-how, it is very easy for us to get sucked into the poisonous realm of instant "likes" and vanity shots that we dread our kids falling victim to. Preaching the evils of these very things can be quite difficult when we are in the process of taking a snap of our best "duck face" and posting it online, but we must let our kids know that these options will be theirs when they are adults; the slippery terrain of social media is slightly less treacherous in later life.

The fact of the matter is, all children love to move, and the majority of the time that they aren't is when we are too tired to do it with them. This is of course a valid reason sometimes, but we need to be conscious of when it spills over from a reason to an excuse. Getting involved in their exercise is a must, and if we constantly find ways to avoid doing it ourselves, then our kids will eventually fall into the same habit.

One of the amazing things about all forms of exercise is that once you begin and the endorphins kick in, you always know that you have made the right choice. Have any of us ever come back from a long walk or an hour at the gym and thought, *I feel a lot worse after that?* The universal answer is "no" because getting up and improving your physical well-being is rewarding in so many ways, and the same applies to children. Remember, they have a lot more energy to burn than us, so helping them to do it will benefit everyone.

When we pique our child's interest in televised sports, the athletes that they see will become intriguing to them, and a need to go outside and replicate what they have seen will encourage them to join a local team or step up their exercise routine. Having sporting idols is a huge part of our childhood, and we should encourage this where possible.

It is no secret that we are our children's first heroes though, and the life lessons that we instill in them will remain throughout their life. The habits and ethics that we pass down contribute a million times more to their makeup than a screen does. Showing them that exercise and a quest for knowledge are privileges and not chores will be fundamental in who they become, so stick *The Wiggles* on the TV and move your butt!

If you want your child to read a book sometimes instead of blasting bad guys on a screen, then find some literature that excites both of your interests. Reading the likes of *Charlotte's Web* together will create the type of bonding moments that are irreplaceable. A nice thing to do is to buy two copies of the book that you wish to read. If your child has their own copy and you read together, they will become a lot more engrossed in the story and on some level, feel that they are living in the grown-up world that seems so magical to them.

Camping trips are a wonderful way to get your child out and about, and there's something so intriguing to your child about the whole thing. Cooking on an open fire and taking in all of the adventure around them will open up a whole new world, and the screens that they adore so much will soon be forgotten. Hey, you can always pretend that you left the tablet behind "by mistake."

When we get out and move with our kids, it is one of the only times that we are truly alone with them. When we leave the background TV and Xbox behind, only conversation and fresh air are left. You will find that your children will open up a lot more when they are facing forward with you and it does not feel like an interrogation room.

As they say, "monkey see, monkey do," and if all our kids witness is their parents slouched in front of the TV or their phone, then they will accept it as the norm and follow suit. Try everything that you can to lead by example and show them that exercise and learning are not only extremely important things, but they can be fun, too.

There will be times when your own screen time will be unavoidable. Some of us work from home, and essentials such as banking are now done online. When this is the case, we have to explain the responsibilities of the real world to our children. When they are very young, all they will see is their parents doing the thing that they forbade them to do. Kids are a lot more understanding than we sometimes give them credit for, so don't be afraid to just tell it like it is.

Screen time is now a part of life, and when we harness it in the right way, it can be an essential tool. Showing our kids how we use it in our grown-up world will prepare them for later life and let them know that tablets and laptops are not just for fun—they can also be used to better yourself, too.

However, try to enjoy your active time with your kids; the next time Instagram makes you feel like a couch potato, then stick the leash on the dog, take your kid by the hand, and step out into the fresh air for some wonderful exercise together.

IF THE COOKIE JAR IS IN REACH, THEY WILL BE EATEN

Unhealthy snacking is a major issue for most parents. Do not think that you're alone in feeling guilty about your child's eating habits. We have all looked on as our kid watches the TV and chows down on a sugary treat and thought, *I really shouldn't have given him that.* Treats are fine when they are used in that very way: as a treat.

When we have a pantry full of easily accessible sugary snacks, then it becomes far too easy for our children to grab a bag of chips or a Twinkie and go to town on them. We all understand how hard it can be to resist the call of a candy bar if we know that all we have to do is walk into the kitchen and open the cupboard. If it is hard for us to resist the temptation, even with everything that we know about the damage they do, then it is going to be a lot harder for our kids.

It is up to us as parents to stock healthy foods and snacks. Of course, we can allow treat days and movie nights, but they have to be controlled, and having a knowledge of what our child eats is massively important. This is not to say that we need to subject them to weekly weigh-ins, but we should have a fair idea of how many healthy meals we have given them that week.

Making up a loose mealtime schedule for our family can help in keeping track of the food that we are all consuming, and help with planning groceries too. Again, this does not have to be overly strict but just making sure that there are more healthy meals than bad ones each week will make us feel a little more secure in the knowledge that everyone in the home is on the right path. Once you get into the routine, it will become a habit, and you will wonder how you ever lived without it.

Much like overloading on the bad things like screen time and sugary snacks is detrimental, eating nothing but broccoli will also do damage in the long run. There is a world of difference between an overly strict diet and a healthy diet. Understanding the differences and how to balance the good with the treats will help in your child's growth and their happiness. None of us should be deprived of some Ben and Jerry's from time to time.

An article by Kate Morin in 2016 pointed out that although a healthy diet is of course essential, overloading our kids on the same "superfoods" can be counterproductive. As strange as it may seem, she noted that too much foods like spinach, beet greens, and Swiss chard can lead to symptoms such as low blood pressure, vomiting, and weak pulse, to name but a few. Although, she does point out that in moderation, they are not only fine, but extremely beneficial.

Canned tuna, she says, although great as part of a healthy diet, can become harmful if it starts being a daily snack, due to the excessive amounts of mercury contained in it. Sticking to the light varieties that consist of the smaller, skipjack tuna, will help. Of course, much like spinach, beet greens, and Swiss chard, having it a few times a week is good for you (Morin, 2016).

This may all seem a little contradictory, given that we are talking about healthy foods being bad, but we are only trying to get across the point that most things in life are harmful when consumed in large amounts.

Screen time should also be viewed in this way, as finding the right balance is important. Being able to use screens in a healthy and productive manner has almost become a survival skill of sorts in the modern age. Almost every career path will involve some form of computer knowledge, and even something as simple as shopping is becoming more and more based in technology. A lot of today's parents grew up on the cusp of this change, yet they still find it hard to grasp the importance of it. Maybe there is still some bomb damage remaining in us from our parents chanting about the dangers of computers—who knows?

Health is intricately linked throughout our whole system, and one part feeds the other. When we are healthy of mind, the idea of exercising or the effort of making a nutritious snack becomes a lot easier. Enthusiasm is ignited, and our life and our perception of the things that had made us anxious shrink a little. When we portray this healthy lifestyle to our children, they will follow our lead and begin to feel the positive effects of looking after themselves.

Preparing healthy treats and meals will make it easier for our kids to grab them from the fridge when they are on the go. Often the thought of having to go to the trouble of making something that takes a while can seem like the effort outweighs the payoff, and the option of just sticking a Pop Tart in the toaster becomes a lot more appealing. If there is a premade rice dish or some carrot sticks sliced in the refrigerator, then your child will not have to wait for the preparation and can enjoy the healthy option immediately instead of eating the unhealthy convenience foods right away.

As we discussed earlier in this chapter, screen time can actually be a useful tool in helping our children to exercise. The apps and games that we mentioned are only a download away, and the benefits that they bring are priceless. Finding a way to incorporate these things into your child's daily routine is easier than you think, and with a little effort from both parties, the energy that they bring will be infectious.

Try and remember that to your child, you are the most amazing human being that they have ever known, so when they see you exercising and choosing a balanced diet, they will be only too happy to do the same.

We will always worry about the effects of the decisions we make for our children—it is unavoidable. However, always know that this is because you are a wonderful parent and that you only want the best for little Johnny and Olivia.

5

ARE SCREENS CAUSING MY CHILD TO BECOME A LONER?

For a lot of parents out there, this can be the single biggest fear surrounding screen time. The thought of allowing our child to become a recluse is one that can cause us extreme anxiety, as the Hollywood image of a forty-year-old loner living in their parent's basement flashes across our mind. The truth of the matter is that connecting with friends— *real* friends— online is just a part of life now.

Of course, when it comes to our kids communicating online, it is always much better and safer if they are doing it with friends from school or the neighborhood. Strangers trying to make contact with our kids is a genuine issue, and vigilance where this is concerned is a must. However, when they are only talking and messaging other children that they are familiar with, then it is only harmless chatting, with the only difference being a headset.

We have already mentioned that being overly strict about our children's online interaction can be detrimental in the long run, but it is something that we really have to hammer home. The majority of the time that your kid is chatting while playing, he/she is doing so with a bunch of his/her buddies from school, and what they are talking about is usually the type of things that all kids do: school, life, girls, boys, TV shows, and everything that they should be chatting about. It's just that it can sometimes be hard for us to look past the screen.

A survey by Monica Anderson and Jingjing Jiang (2018) found that nearly 51% of teenagers and children in the U.S. claimed that they had no real problems when it came to fitting into social circles. This is a skill that is believed to be rapidly dying out because of online gaming and screen time, yet the numbers are basically the same as they always have been.

Further, 49% of kids and teens said that they found it harder than most to fit in (Anderson & Jiang, 2018). This sounds like a high percentage, but in truth, it is no different than every schoolyard or social event in the world 50 years ago. Some kids just find it easier to feel comfortable in crowds, while others struggle—screen time or not.

This same study also showed that 35% of teens claimed that some of their closest friends not only lived on the other side of the country, but some of them lived in *different* countries (Anderson & Jiang, 2018). This is not only a high number, it is a whole new phenomenon, and the amount of multicultural, multiracial friendships that are being formed today have never been as high. Not only is this a new beginning in many ways, but it is also a wonderful thing to be celebrated. Social media and screen time, for all of its faults, have some truly amazing gifts to be cherished when we look at it with an open mind.

Also, 88% of these teens were said to spend at least one day a week online with their friends, while 77% said that they would manage the same amount, if not more, face-to-face. These numbers are a lot closer than the media would have us believe, and when distance, weather, homelife, and many other aspects are taken into account, it is downright impressive (Anderson & Jiang, 2018).

Kids these days are a lot busier than they have ever been. This is in part due to the instant reaction and fast-paced world of social media and technology in general, but it doesn't take away from the fact that the world in which our children live leaves them with less time to just "hang out." Sometimes, the only way they can let off steam and socialize with their friends is by going online and bonding.

There are times that even when our children are laughing and joking into their headsets when we can still let the fear of them becoming loners creep into our thoughts. Even though they are clearly communicating with many of their friends, somehow we let the thought remain that they are on their own, when what they are doing is no different from talking to someone on the phone.

Online communication will never replace face-to-face interaction, but allowing them to have some daily fun with their friends while they play Xbox for an hour, will only strengthen the bonds that they are creating and will lead to stronger and healthier relationships. If they are the only ones not allowed to play, then it is almost like being grounded in a way, as they sit there miserable with all the thoughts of the fun their friends are having without them playing in their mind.

English as a Second Language (ESL) kids can bond over video games, and the English that is being spoken all around them will sink in naturally, just as immersing ourselves in another culture will help us in learning. This also applies to kids who move from a different area or country. The level playing field of an online platform and the easily accessible options to tag friends and join in will make fitting in and bonding a whole lot easier. Sometimes, a child who starts in a new school will find it hard enough to find the time to talk to others, let alone build up real friendships. Blasting their way through *Fortnite* with the other kids or being tagged in a funny video can sometimes be just the thing they need to bond.

One of our main concerns is that the relationships our child is building online are not "real" friends. This is not true, and as mentioned earlier, most of the time it is friends from school that they are playing with. Playground chats these days are more about online ratings and viral videos than trading cards or who is around to play "stickball" by the fire hydrant until the last light. What our kids—and everyone else's—are running home for is to continue building the *Minecraft* world they created with their friend. Remember, they have been excited about it all day, and an hour with their best pal online won't do any harm.

The hard part for most of us can be understanding that bonding online is just a way of life now. We are all standing directly at the turning point of the technological age, and the screams from both ends of the argument can be deafening. When our children's health is at risk, or at least perceived to be, it can be extremely hard for us to make a concrete decision on what is best. On the one hand, we want our kids to be happy and have a good network of friends, but on the other hand, we don't want to still be washing Cheeto dust off their Hawaiian shirts in their 40s.

Luckily, if we educate ourselves a little on the pluses of screen time and the friendships for our kids that it can strengthen, then we can begin to accept that there are some benefits to it. We just have to keep an eye on the amount of time they do it and make sure that they are still getting out of the house on a regular basis. Let's face it: When we retire, we would like to use the basement for more than big Johnny's gaming room.

SCREEN TIME FOR CHILDREN WITH AUTISM AND SPECIAL NEEDS

Screen time can be an essential part of raising our children, especially under certain circumstances. Some children with autism will find that computer games or YouTube videos sync better with their attention than face-to-face interaction.

My teenage niece has autism. She connects through screens and is very interested in not just computer games but the intricacies in how they are made and the inner workings of them. Like many people with autism, regular conversations are tough for her, but through her screen, she has been able to make connections and build games. Learning about computer programming and going at her own pace has been very significant for her, she is also able to draw on screens and make cartoons which has led to her sharing her art with others online. This, in turn, leads to her wanting to converse more about what she has learned and created in person.

Often, kids and adults with learning difficulties or special needs can find computer games and online interaction a great leveler. The connections that they can make with other people can last a lifetime, and the inclusive nature of all-in online games such as *Fortnite* and *Minecraft* provide a wonderful world for friends to engage each other no matter where they are in the world.

Researcher Julie Peake, in her fantastic article, "Screen Time for Children on the Autism Spectrum," said that screen time for both autistic and neurotypical children should be basically the same amount, but a little more leniency should be allowed for children on the spectrum (Peake, 2018).

She goes on to point out that many autistic children and adults alike, find the joy of screens and gaming to be relaxing, as the predictive and repetitive interface is more suited to their neurological makeup. It can make them feel a little more in control of their surroundings (Peake, 2018).

The visuals and sounds of a video they are familiar with can stimulate the neural pathways and bring a calmness and comfort that sometimes cannot be achieved with a one-on-one conversation. These are all things that should be considered when we are raising kids that are faced with these difficulties.

Peake finishes by assuring us that many surveys have been done on the subject of screen time for kids on the spectrum, and in general, they tend to spend a bit more time online than their neurotypical peers (Peake, 2018). With that in mind, do not feel bad for allowing your child some extra YouTube moments or Xbox play.

Life is hard enough as a parent. Sometimes we need to just let go and enjoy the moment without overthinking things. A life of being constantly "on" is exhausting, and although we all want what is best for our kids, this can sometimes mean turning a blind eye to that extra hour online or the rewatching of some mundane video. Our happiness is a vital part of our children's lives too, and if letting them have a "free day" every once in a while means that we get to take a nap or watch some of our own trashy TV, then smile, give them a hug, and find out what the girls are up to on *The View.*

Freedom to relax a little when raising kids is something that we all need to accept as fact and not a guilty pleasure. Parents who are raising children with special needs or are on the spectrum need to understand that they are doing an amazing job. Often, there is not enough credit given to these wonderful people, and they need to understand that taking a break for a while to do something that they enjoy does not make them any less of a parent—it only makes them human. We all need a little time to ourselves to detoxify, as it is fundamental to our well-being.

Fearing that screen time is making our child into a loner can be intensified when they have any of the issues that we have mentioned, but as we also discussed, sometimes the screen is the time where they bond the most. It can not only be a place where they meet their friends and make new ones, but it can also be one of the only social settings where they feel a little at ease. This should only be encouraged and if someone you know rolls their eyes, then cut them out of your life in five minutes and forget them in the next 10. Nobody understands your kids the way you do, so you are the one that knows what is best.

Although screen time has positive effects on bonding and creating relationships, as always, we must still be very aware of when it slips from fun into an addiction. Dragging your child back from the comfortable world of the screen when they start to use it as an escape can be extremely difficult, and nipping it in the bud early on will help in creating boundaries and an understanding in your child that too much screen time will be damaging. Find some fun, stimulating activities to substitute in or books that you can both enjoy.

There are also things like *special interest forums* and groups that your child can join, which are basically just discussion rooms or book clubs. These amazing sites not only encourage interaction on a calm and friendly level, but they will tweak your child's interest in other subjects and build friendships, too. Another plus to these forums is that the interests discussed in them may not be shared by your child's peers, especially if it is something advanced or out of the general interests of kids their age. These specialist sites surround them with like-minded individuals who only want to share a similar passion.

There are many apps and games that we can use as productive tools in our children's life. We just need to figure out which ones suit us best, and set our limits on the times spent playing them.

JUST BECAUSE THEY ARE PLAYING ALONE, DOES NOT MEAN THEY *ARE* ALONE

We sometimes need to remember that when our child is online and chatting away into their headset, all of their friends are on the other end. It is very easy for us to imagine that they are lost in a world of their own and losing touch with the people in the real world. This is not always the case, and as we all now know, the online invitation is the new doorbell ring.

Before computer games became linked worldwide through the wonders of online gaming, the fear of screen time consumption was a much more valid worry. It is still an issue, of course, but the days of one-player games with zero interaction have all but faded away. Games now call for hundreds of players at a time, and more often than not, your child will partake in this with a bunch of their pals. Even games for the younger kids, such as *Roblox*, have chat options for the little ones to send messages to their friends. Not only are they communicating, they are typing messages and learning the valuable lesson of online interaction that is bound to be an aspect of whatever career they choose in later life.

Most online gamers will tell you that the time that they spend online with their existing friends only strengthens the bonds and closeness that they feel with them. Meeting buddies in a game is just one of the ways in which kids hang out now, and depriving them of this will only lead to exclusion and heartache.

When we find a healthy amount of time for them to play online, then everyone can rest easy knowing that they haven't overdone it, and they still had a chance to hang out with their friends.

Outside of school, today's child spends more time online with their friends than in person. As scary as this statistic may seem to us, we need to recognize that it is not only in our household that it is happening but all around the world. It is a part of life, and like anything that comes along like this, we find it hard to contemplate and feel that it can be detrimental to our children, we need to become more knowledgeable in the positive and negative aspects, and make a game plan.

Kids often grow out of gaming—that is always something that we need to keep in mind. Like any craze when we were kids, the appeal of something popular in our youth can vanish as we grow older, and if they don't, then make them wash the Cheeto dust off their *own* Hawaiian shirt!

The world is linked now. From our iPads and Alexa, we can pretty much find out anything we want or even pay all of our bills and do the shopping without ever leaving the house. This is the only life that our kids have ever known. Their understanding of why they cannot use them all the time can be hard for them to perceive, and we must explain that they are not only for fun but for real life, too.

Try to put yourself in their shoes sometimes. When all of their friends are engaged in a game or an online discussion and we forbid them from joining in, they will naturally feel left out and excluded. Of course, we cannot give in to their every whim, as that will lead to them becoming that screeching kid we see at the mall who smashes the place up until they get what they want, and nobody wants that. However, bending our rules from time to time when the moment calls for it will do no harm, and your kid will be very grateful for it.

One extremely important thing that we must teach our children is that Facebook friends and YouTube followers are not akin to real friends—at least not in the sense of the amount of them and how close they actually are. They will have their close friends on social media, sure, but when the numbers start going into the hundreds, they must be made to understand that Mikey's friend of a friend that they met once at a playdate, might not even recognize them if they passed them at McDonald's. This is not being harsh, it is just a fact of life, and in knowing these things, they will not grow up in a world where they feel that they must please everyone all the time to maintain hundreds of "friendships."

The time your child spends online *can* be productive. Not just in the educational games and apps that we discussed, but in the online worlds of *Fortnite*, *Roblox*, and endless others, too. The friends that they interact with are the ones that will be there throughout their lives, they are just bonding in a way that is a little alien to us.

Even us adults could learn a thing or two from our kids when it comes to the world of online gaming and the "headset." How often have we sent a meaningless text to a friend or relation instead of calling them and having a real conversation? When our kids are interacting through their microphone, they are at least verbally communicating, and as we hear the laughter and joy that comes from their bedroom as they play, it can be very hard to remember what we were mad about in the first place.

6

AM I ALLOWING MY CHILD TO
WASTE TIME?

The first thing that we should always look at is that there is a very good chance the amount of time that your child is spending gaming or watching videos on YouTube is probably not as much as you think. By that, we mean the period in which they are online is no different and could even be less than average.

As hard as it can be for us to grasp, time online is not always time wasted. Even the type of games we have mentioned before —*Fortnite, Black Ops*, and the like—can still have some beneficial effects. The reactions used, communication, teamwork, bonding, social skills, are all things that will help our child in the long run. The basis of a lot of our fears is sometimes lost in the endless horror stories and warnings that we see on social media. More often than not, these posts are completely unfounded and are just the opinions of one parent.

When we take into account all of the educational games that we have discussed, we can start to let go of the stigma attached to screens and begin to understand that controlled screen time is not only fun for our kids, but it can help them, too. Letting them navigate and learn their way through the technological world which will be so heavily influential when they grow up can only be a good thing.

Endless studies have been done on the positive and negative effects of screen time on kids, but with rapidly changing games, phones, streaming services, and trends, the findings can become almost redundant by the time the ink dries. Keeping up with the advances and information as much as possible ourselves will lend us a hand when it comes to deciding how much time is spent online and what games should be played.

The reality is that some kids are spending too much time on screens—it is an unavoidable truth. What needs to be remembered though, is that for most kids it is probably a lot less than you think. Chances are that your child falls into the category of "just enough." If this is not the case, and you feel that they are spending way too much time online, then you will need to step in and put some restrictions in place.

On the other hand, if you are starting to see that your initial fears were maybe just a little rash, then staying on top of things as you have been doing thus far will be a good start in keeping them on the right track. In knowing that they are not doing any irreparable damage, you should find a little more peace of mind when they fire up the PlayStation or tablet each day.

The term "wasting time" throws up images of a zombie-like child staring blankly at a rapidly moving screen with chip bags and empty pizza boxes strewn all over the room, and of course, there will be days when this image is almost real. However, haven't we done the same in front of the TV or our phone? We need to know that most of the time, whether it is a FPS online with their friends, or a repetitive YouTube video that our toddler just loves, what they are doing will have at least some positives attached.

Minecraft has been talked about in many scientific circles as a big plus when it comes to our child's growth.

A study from the University of Glasgow in 2017 found that games such as *Minecraft* in early life are linked to future benefits in education and college graduation. These games were shown to increase creativity, adaptability, communication, and resource skills—all things that are fundamental in our growth and career paths.

Building a *Minecraft* world from scratch not only takes all the skills we just listed, but it also requires patience. This is one of the most important traits that any person can acquire, especially in the fast-paced world we live in today. Laying each individual block and waiting days, sometimes weeks, for your creation to be completed is something that even the most well-adjusted adults would struggle to do. Watching our child build something from nothing is a beautiful thing, regardless of the fact that they did it on a screen.

When *Minecraft* and other games are played in a multiplayer mode, your child will be strengthening existing friendships as they also learn the importance of teamwork. Creating something with another is extremely rewarding, much as sharing in their joy is too. Just because we do not have the tangible results of what they have built in our hands as we would with Lego does not make it any less impressive in the grand scheme of things.

Patience and perseverance are so important, and if these games can help build these strengths in our kids, then we have to allow ourselves to accept them as such. They will all have negatives involved too, of course, but concentrating on the positives from time to time does no harm.

In Eric Mack's 2019 article for Forbes, he puts our mind at ease by letting us know that according to recent studies, it was found that one or two hours of screen time a day is actually good for children.

The study that he cites was carried out with a questionnaire that was given to 35,000 parents and caregivers by Professor Andrew Przybylski, the Director of Research at the Oxford Internet Institute.

What was discovered was that these parents and caregivers admitted to their kids being online for an average of one hour and 53 minutes a day. Of course, we must not take this as read, and by that we mean it is probably more. Who among us hasn't sugarcoated the amount of time our children spend online when discussing it with other parents? Even with ourselves (Mack, 2019).

He also points out that the findings showed that it took up to five hours of nonstop screen time before the children showed significant signs of functional difficulties (Mack, 2019). This is by no means suggesting that five hours a day of L.O.L. Surprise videos or *Fortnite* are healthy—far from it—it is only to say that our kids have a much stronger tolerance to it than we imagine.

The article finishes by referring back to Przybylski's study, and the finding that one or two hours a day of online interaction increased the children's social skills, emotional well-being, and peace of mind.

Sometimes what we see as time wasted where our kids are concerned is in truth time well spent, especially through their eyes. We just need to learn when to let it go a little and when to put our foot down: hopefully not on an empty pizza box or chip bag!

EMOTIONAL INTELLIGENCE

Emotional Intelligence (EQ) in our children is vitally important. Empathy and care for others are something that we should always encourage. As much as we all strive to instill these beliefs and standards in our little ones, there are also an array of TV shows that can help us with the process.

- *Daniel Tiger's Neighborhood*
- *Curious George*
- *Maya the Bee*
- *Franny's Feet*
- *Clangers*
- *Nina's World*
- *Super Wings*
- *Llama Llama*
- *Tinga Tinga Tales*

These are just some of the fantastic programs out there that are aimed at giving toddlers and young kids a helping hand in learning how to be kind to others. Lessons and ethics are all part of the colorful way in which they are delivered, and a lot of them will involve dancing or movement of some kind.

Many of the shows on TV and YouTube are a wonderful way for your young kids to prepare for preschool too, as many of the subjects covered will come up in the first years of schooling. For children with no siblings, it can be a great way to encourage sharing and being part of a group.

When we allow our children to partake in these EQ-based shows, we are helping them with their growth and letting them see a world where kindness and empathy are engrained. The colors and movement—especially where toddlers are concerned —are vital in their progression, and as they progress to the slightly more advanced shows, counting and reading are introduced. They are done in such a casual and friendly way that it can be hard for us to see it sometimes, but it is all there for them.

Emotional intelligence is normally a given in children. It is only later in life as the world around us starts to sharpen our edges that it can take a bit of a knock. These shows and videos only aim to strengthen the empathy that already exists in our kids and teach them that giving and sharing is fun and not something to be viewed as a negative. Preparing them for the trials and tribulations of early school life and later adulthood can only be positive, and learning to share and care for others is an asset.

We are often led to believe that allowing our kids to watch TV is an awful thing to do—that it "rots their brain" or makes them unresponsive to our rules. This, as always, only applies to massive amounts of screen time, and when the time we allow is spent watching EQ-based shows or apps, then we can give ourselves a bit of a break in knowing that they are learning as they watch. If it gives us a little time to watch some trash ourselves or call our friends for a chitchat, then all the better.

Many of these shows will also encourage arts and crafts. At these times, our kids are learning to create and work with their hands. Feelings of accomplishment and the joys of a job well done will all be instilled by whatever they create, and the projects that require the help of an adult will teach teamwork and patience, for both parties.

When you can, sit through some of these shows with your little one. If we pay enough attention, we can begin to see all of the benefits that they bring. The kindness that they teach is wonderful, and acceptance is the basis of most, if not all, of them. When we learn to take them for what they are— helpful — we allow ourselves a bit of slack, and the stick that we use to beat ourselves with becomes a little bit softer.

It is only natural for parents to question the decisions that they make concerning the well-being of their children—we all do it, and we always will do it. It is one of the burdens of raising a child. What we are trying to do here is to take away some of the negativity attached to screen time and let the reader know that when they harness it in the correct ways, the results can be amazing. One of the main issues can be our perspective on the whole thing. Once we adjust it a little and understand that everything about technology and screen time isn't detrimental, then a lot of the worries and anxiety we had, fades away.

So, when your kid is watching Daniel Tiger do his thing, or Curious George getting lost in the big city once again, try to let yourself relax a little in knowing that their empathy and kindness are all that is being encouraged, and it is being done so in a sweet and positive manner.

KIDS NEED TO UNWIND, TOO

When we get in from a hard day's work, we like nothing better than to kick our shoes off, make a snack, and flop down onto the couch. That audible sigh that we let out at finally being home to our comfortable surroundings is one of the sweetest feelings in the world. Knowing that we will not hear the *bleep* of another email that morning or the *ping* of the bell as another order of eggs over easy gets rang in frees our mind and allows us to begin letting the stresses of the day slip away.

Our kids are no different. When we view their school time in the same manner, it is a little easier to understand that they just spent half the day reading, learning, and studying—all things that we are sure they would have preferred not to do. The thought of plugging in with their buddies at the end of the day is probably one of the things that got them through it.

Allowing them to kick back for a couple of hours does not make you a lazy parent, only understanding. We must remember that kids spend the best part of their day doing what they are told: When to get up, when to go to school, what subject they are studying, when to have their lunch break, and the list goes on and on. Even once they get home, they have homework, family time, and chores before they are told when to go back to bed so they can start all over again in the morning. There are only so many minutes in the day, and we have to allow them some time to unwind. If going online with their friends or watching a YouTube video is how they relax, then it seems a bit counter-productive to deny them this.

Video games, as a whole, have a goal to aim for if you are to succeed in them. Unwittingly or not, these traits that your child is learning will teach them to be successful in life and to aim for the top. It will help them by learning that if you take a project on and finish it, the rewards are there at the end. It may seem superficial to word it this way, but it is all fact. These skills, and many like them, are instilled in online gaming.

This is touched on in Mark Rober's TED Talk, where he points to the Super Mario Effect, in which he and his buddies growing up would race to school to discuss how far they got in the game (Rober, 2015). If they heard that they weren't as far as a friend, they didn't just give up. They worked harder at it to achieve the ultimate goal of rescuing the Princess from the castle of the evil Bowser. There is a determination to these games, and the traits that some of them can give our kids can be priceless.

Unwinding and relaxing with apps such as Facetime are not only wonderful ways for our children to communicate, but they encourage interaction that is essentially face-to-face. The communicative skills they learn will be essential in future online work and job interviews, as the back and forth of the conversations will become a natural part of your child's life.

There are times when we can unintentionally overwhelm our children with "too much of a good thing." By this, we mean constantly coming up with new active and trendy ways to entertain them.

Getting them out of the house for nature walks and sporting events are massively important, but when we break down their day like we did earlier in this section and realize that they have an awful lot of things to do in their daily routine, we can sometimes creep into overload territory, which leaves them with little or no time to do the one thing that they find truly relaxing. Much like finding a balance on the amount of time spent on screens, we also have to be a little wary of too many activities but only a little, as outdoor fun and family time is so important, no matter how much of a fuss they kick up.

Another roadblock in viewing their online gaming as "relaxing" is just how hectic and fast-paced the games can seem. We have all stood there watching our child's hands moving at what seems like a blur, as the character on the screen moves rapidly from one level to the next, and thought, *That cannot be relaxing for them.* Amazingly enough, it actually is. It is their time with their pals and their time to unwind.

As hard as it is for us to view it this way, there have been many studies that have shown the neurological benefits of FPS and online gaming. The brain is constantly being challenged and worked, and the fast-paced action mixed with the constant verbal interaction helps with multitasking and dealing with pressure situations. The ability to remain calm under severe difficulty is not something that many people can achieve. If a little online battle helps to improve our child's ability to do so, then we should try to encourage it but only for a certain amount of time each day.

Remember that we need to let them have a little downtime when we can because as strange as it can sometimes seem, the rapid moving of fingers and the endless explosions on the screen is just them kicking back on the couch and sipping tea, and we all know how important it is to relax after a long day.

7

ARE SCREENS TURNING MY CHILD INTO A CRIMINAL?

We have touched on this in the "Video Games and Violence" section of Chapter One, but violence in video games and its links to real-life crime is such a hot topic that we really must look at it from all angles. A game such as *Grand Theft Auto,* a blend of both shooter and racing games, has ironically been used as a stick to beat the life out of the issue of violence among children for decades, and it is very easy to watch these games play out and link them firmly to crime and violence.

However, we must remember that these problems have always been around, and long before video games, the anger people felt was at an array of other things, including movies, music, and literature. Book burnings have been popular throughout history, as the spark of one person's issue can ignite and spread through the whole community as they protest the "evils" of George Orwell's *Nineteen Eighty-Four.*

Now, we are by no means putting on-screen violence on the same level as a genius work by Orwell, but we have to consider the tolerance factor and the inescapable truth that kids these days will see and hear of a lot more violence than they did in the past. Unless we plan on raising them under a rock, then the chances of them seeing a video on YouTube or playing a video game with violence in it are unfortunately extremely high—almost inevitable.

As hard as it is to accept, violence is a part of life, and as we have tried to accomplish throughout this book, we must learn to take the positives from every situation. "Positives in violence?" I hear you ask—and rightly so. If we open our minds to the acceptance that it is unavoidable, we can begin to make a concrete game plan to deal with it.

Even if protests and bans on certain games were somewhat successful, the opportunity to play them or to get access to videos would still always remain. If anything, much like the "Parental Advisory" stickers on CDs in the 90s, the intrigue of a banned game would be what becomes the most appealing factor to our child. This is just a part of growing up and believing that if you are told not to do something, then it must be good.

When we give in to the knowledge that there is violence in video games and online, we can start to talk openly to our children about it. Teaching them the difference between what they see on the screen and what is acceptable in real life will help them to understand that what they are seeing is just a bunch of moving pixels. They will understand that the violence shown in these games is not applicable to real life.

Although many of these games have an age limit, they will still be longed for by your child. In no way should you let an infant play games such as *GTA* or *Among Us*, but as they hit their teen years, we need to relent a little and edge these things in if it is what they desire. Shielding and excluding them from such games will only leave them behind their friends, and as we mentioned already, the appeal of what they are forbidden to do will become a carrot that they will walk off a cliff to chomp down.

FPS and driving games are actually proven to be the most effective in boosting cognitive function, so as hard as it may be for us to accept, games like *GTA*, that involve shooting and driving, will probably be the most beneficial where this trait is concerned. Again, this is only one of the positives stacked up against several negatives. It is how we view them and the rules we lay down that will be the deciding factor on how these games reflect on our children's upbringing.

It is very easy for us to jump on the violence in video games when our child throws a tantrum or snatches a toy from another kid at the park. The same goes for when our teenage son blows the bangs out of the eyes that you haven't seen in two years and says, "Shut up, Mom." The truth is most, if not all, of these reactions were formed by the real-life events that they see going on around them. Kids are a lot more likely to follow the example of a parent or friend than they are of something they have seen on a screen. If that wasn't the case, then the kids that came before would have been riding Acme rockets around or sticking their finger in the socket to light up like Pikachu.

How we explain TV violence and age-appropriate games to our children will be the most important factor, and of course, having a cutoff point on the amount of time played will be an all-important mention. Much more detrimental damage is caused by marathon screen time than the games they play. It is just far too easy for us to blame the content when little Johnny or Olivia kick up a fuss.

Kids will learn to act up if they are unhappy even when they are still in the cradle. It is ingrained in us as human beings, and they have done it since the beginning of time. It is not a real issue, as we as parents know how to explain to them that it is wrong as soon as they start to understand us and hopefully we can outmaneuver them early on.

Nobody wants their child to become a criminal or a violent person, and the things that they see on screen can be horrific at times. However, when we raise them to know the difference and we understand that shielding them from it is not an option, it becomes just another thing that we have to teach them. Much like explaining to them not to put their hand on the stove when they begin to walk, instilling the beliefs in ethics and kindness is just as important in their growth. The difference between screen violence and how to behave in the real world is just another one that we have to teach.

THE STUDIES

An almost endless array of studies has been carried out on the links to video games and violence. Even before the horrors of Columbine, the debate had raged over what influence these games were having on the youth. Both sides probably *do* have an argument, but neither one can prove conclusively that they are correct. If anything, until there is solid scientific and psychological evidence from the side of the doubters, then the people who claim that the violence on screen is not to blame for the world's problems, kind of have the upper hand.

In a *Wall Street Journal* article by Julie Jargon in 2021, she alludes to this fact. She confirms that although thousands of studies have been carried out on the links between video games and real-life violence, no direct correlation has been conclusively proven. This only really proves that the argument from both sides is quite subjective at the moment and pretty much shows that the decisions we make on how often our kids go online and what they play and see is still up for debate.

Jargon goes on to point out that U.S. consumers spent a whopping 19 billion dollars on video games in the fourth quarter of

2020, which was up a massive 26% from the previous year. This of course had a lot to do with the pandemic and everybody's need to stay indoors, but the fact is that gaming is here to stay, and the easily accessible nature of downloadable games, will make it even harder to control what our children play (Jargon, 2021).

When we look at studies on topics such as this one, we have to try and remember that the technological world in which we live is so rapidly changing. The first iPhone is barely 15 years old, which is a pretty hard thing to fathom, as it feels like it has been around forever. Now, this does not mean that because it is 15 it is going to start snapping answers back to us and listening to Slayer—it only puts into perspective the speed at which things change. This is why a lot of these studies and research can become redundant quite quickly, as access to videos and games is ever-changing.

Long gone are the days when our dial-up Internet took half an hour to fire up before we waited another hour for the picture they may or may not be Pamela Anderson to download. Now, if kids want to show their friends some unsavory video or link them to particularly gory online FPS, they only have to swipe a screen and it is there. Trying to remain endlessly vigilant on this is impossible and exhausting. Teaching our kids about reality early on is a lot more important.

From a neurological point of view, Philip M. Boffey writes in the defense of video game violence.

He points out that although the amount of game time to population the world over is the same, other countries do not have to deal with the mass shootings and daily violence that occurs in the United States. In fact, he points out that the discrepancy in crime rates all over the world vary quite greatly (Boffey, 2019).

Boffey then quotes a 2017 statement from the American Psychological Department (APA), in which they found "scant evidence" in the connection between violence and video games and "little evidence" linking it to criminal behavior (Boffey, 2019).

In Jane McGonigal's mind-blowing TED Talk, she breaks down the traits and skills that are involved in being a serious gamer. She tells us that the urgency needed to start a mission straight away, will only lead to a determination and a belief in avoiding procrastination (McGonigal, 2010).

This will in turn becomes a need to tackle any obstacles that come their way and see the job out until the end. Determination, hard work, and dedication are all needed to start, maintain, and complete most video games.

McGonigal (2010) lightens the mood by referring to the "hope" that is needed. The sprawling alien worlds or endless tracks in today's video games take a certain type of hopeful individual—a dreamer, so to speak. This is not in the negative sense, but someone who believes that anything is possible if they put their mind and effort into completing a task.

The "social fabric" created with their friends and fellow gamers, she points out, will instill trust, bonding, reliability, and teamwork: all things that are needed when embarking on a mission or the creation of an online world. Putting your trust in someone else's passion to see something out with you requires extreme loyalty and faith in others.

Many times, when video game violence is the hot topic on all of the news channels after a tragic shooting or a rise in crime, it is a deflection tactic used to point the blame away from other real, more serious issues. The root of violence in humans goes far deeper and a lot further back than *GTA*.

Studies in topics such as this can only bring us so far, as there will always be valid arguments from both camps, and trying to decide on the right path to allow our kids to walk can be heartbreaking. However, if we have raised them as best we can in knowing the differences between right and wrong, then allowing them a little game time here and there will have no negative effects.

As much as we would love some conclusive evidence to be found from either side, the likelihood of this occurring is slim. This is only because it is so hard to prove. Video game violence will always be around, and laying down rules and beliefs is the best defense we have against it.

WHAT YOUR CHILD IS REALLY PLAYING

Children and adults of all ages are playing *Fortnite*. We have referred to this online craze several times throughout this book and with good reason. Although the makers of the game claim that it is aimed at ages 12 and above, we all know full well that this is far from the truth. If this was the case, then the company would not be producing *Fortnite* T-shirts in small and colorful pencil cases, school bags, action figures, and every other gimmick imaginable.

These products are aimed at young kids, and that is okay. *Fortnite*, although set in a world where the object is to kill everyone around you, has zero blood and the action is colorful and harmless. Or course, for some parents, this sugary packaging is not enough, and the on-screen violence is still all that remains. No one here can tell another parent how to raise their child. It is akin to feeding someone else's kids sweets when they have specifically requested that you don't. All we can do here is lay down a thesis, and allow each parent to make their own decision on what is good for their little ones and what is not.

The world of *Fortnite* is a social hub, too. Often, when a player has been eliminated, they will not even join back in for a while and just continue chatting with their friends. A lot of the time, the action on the screen becomes secondary, and the "hanging out" is what the main goal is. When this occurs, it basically just becomes a group chat with some action in the background.

Many people will claim that violence is violence, no matter how much lipstick you plaster on its face. This is true, of course, but the intention and level of it should be taken into consideration sometimes. How it is depicted can make a world of difference, and when stacked up against the adult-based worlds of *GTA* and other such games, it is not very far removed from watching the likes of *Spiderman* or *PJ Masks*, both of which contain light violence, but in a colorful way.

Often, allowing your child to play a lighter FPS like *Fortnite* can be a fair trade for the copy of *GTA* that they really want. This is not said to promote giving in to your child's demands, it is only to say that sometimes a little give and take is important. The last thing we want is our kids knowing that they can "tantrum" us into giving them anything they want.

Much like *Fortnite* can be a nice substitute for the FPS aspect of games like *GTA*, *Mario Kart* is a wonderful way to fill in the gaping wound left by us removing the driving aspect of it. There is action in *Mario Kart*, sure, but it is so diluted that you will barely taste it, and the family aspect of this game is a massive plus, as adults can enjoy it just as much.

Minecraft, when you break it down, has violence in it, too. Zombies, creepers, spiders, endermen, and many more can be cracked across the head and killed with clubs and swords. It is the basic graphics and fun nature of the game that stops us from becoming alarmed, but we all know that *Minecraft* is a fantastic game. Not just in the fun it brings, but in all the other wonderful beneficial ways that we have mentioned earlier in the book. The fact that a few cube-faced skeletons get a whack every now and then does not take away from all of the positives that it brings.

Just like *Fortnite*, most of these games are played online these days, and that opens up the "community" aspect that we touched on. These are the places where your children strengthen existing friendships and begin new ones. Allowing ourselves to concentrate on the communicative side of it will at least relieve some of the stress and anxiety.

Remember, talk to your child about the games they play. It doesn't have to be a serious discussion (we have already had that) but just an interest in how they got on or what parts they enjoyed. You will begin to see that it is never the violence that they concentrate on. Sure, they will mention how many "kills" they got, but it is just another way of saying "points." Talking to them will allow you to gain insight into what parts of these games they are truly interested in.

Letting ourselves spend some time in our child's world opens the door to understanding. Partaking in the joys they receive from these games is a great leveler, and once we can let go of the stigma attached, we can see the experience for what it really is to them: just a bit of a get-together with their friends. If it gets a little competitive from time to time, then so be it; they are learning a skill. If the constant squeals from the room cut through our heads like a blade, well, they are just having fun. If you enter the room and they introduce themselves, then no—it is time to turn it off!

Substituting games is a good tool to have. Slipping some of the educational games or EQ-based apps that we have covered sometimes is a sure way for everyone to be roughly on the same page. Video games are not always a bad thing—it can just be hard at times to move past the explosions.

8

HOW CAN I USE SCREEN TIME TO MY ADVANTAGE?

There are many ways to achieve the answer to this question. From pointing them in the direction of educational games and apps to understanding what they are actually doing during their screen time. Many of these points we have touched on already, but reinforcing them to our children, and ourselves, will help in finding a new and better technological middle ground with our little ones.

Using screen time to your advantage can be often easier with our younger children. Many of the games and apps that they already enjoy are educational by nature. With our toddlers and kiddos, the passive videos that they watch can actually be more detrimental than certain games, as the option to just zone out is much easier. When they have a game or an app that needs their attention, the neurological effort that it takes will keep their brains active.

The rewarding "achievements" and playful sounds of these games encourage our kids to push on to try and better themselves. When we are small, gratification from anyone but our parents, even a digitally created bear with glasses on, feels a lot more rewarding. Unfortunately, for us supportive and loving parents, saying, "Well done" to our child begins to lose its effect in their minds after a while but never stop—this is only because you are Mom and Dad, and it is your duty to be supportive! They know this, and the expectancy is always there.

It's there around the time when, "Leave me alone, Mom," and "I AM switching it off, Dad" comes into play. When every suggestion is met with a scoff or a grunted answer, and you are led to believe by someone who has spent 14 years on the planet that everything you thought you knew is "so wrong," we can begin to try and become more observant of the actual screen time that is being consumed.

By this, we don't mean spying on their every move—such things will only lead to distrust and our child feeling constantly watched. What we need to do is be more vigilant in knowing if it is passive or active time being spent. Often, when our kid is on Instagram, they are posting extremely artful pictures that they spent a lot of time changing filters and reworking into something that they are proud of, yet they're shy about showing to their folks or people that they know. When they can anonymously post them on a page that is solely for the purpose of aspiring photographers, they can relax a little in knowing that any criticism will not be made face-to-face. They will come out of their shell eventually if we give them some space.

Understanding what our teens and tweens are doing online does not involve going through their search history. Talking to them in a casual and calm manner will help them to open up and let us in a little. These moments of bonding are so important, and they can be the type of thing that opens up a whole new world of closeness between you both. Try not to be too critical of whichever hobby it is they are enjoying, as comments like, "There is no money in that" will only hurt their feelings and prove to them that you "just don't get it."

Setting boundaries for screen time and the type of game and video being watched is a lot easier with our younger kids. They will always be a lot more responsive to our rules and regulations, and when told to turn it off, they will react accordingly more often than not.

With our older kids, this can be a little tricky, and shutting the Wi-Fi down at certain times can be the best way to do it. There might be some huffing and puffing, but they will get over it. Just be careful to understand that the game they are involved in with their friends is in progress when you tell them to turn off the computer, so be a little patient and let them finish up before losing your cool.

An interesting article by Hiniker et al. (2016) covers some of these issues and finds that although the transitioning away from screens can be difficult, predictive factors determine the pain of transition. Meaning that if kids know in advance, then they are more likely to accept the shut off time. The study also found that technology-based transitions were significantly more successful than parent-mediated transitions suggesting that since there is no one to argue with children just accept the boundaries and respect the limits.

In the survey of around 250 parents and their kids across the United States, studying the effects and problems that arise with conflict over screen time or "restricted meditation," they found some other very interesting facts that may help put your mind at ease a little.

The results of this survey showed that most older kids, between 10–17, were much more receptive to the rule of cutting out certain apps and games over removing tablets and computers in certain contexts; by this, they mean phones or tablets at the dinner table and the like. When faced with the choice of either of these, the kids would have much rather eliminated Snapchat from their lives than have to put the phone away completely (Hiniker et al., 2016).

This has a lot to do with the instant reply and social media world that we now reside in and only goes to solidify the point we made earlier in the book: It is oftentimes more the "missing out" on things with their friends that is the real issue. When viewed this way, we can very easily humanize the need for tablets and phones, as we all know what it is like to feel excluded. Every single one of us, big or small, has watched sweaty-palmed for the Emily "is typing . . ." icon to come alive when we are waiting on a reply to something important.

What this article also alluded to, was that most of the kids believed that they would be more receptive to these rules if they didn't have to watch their parents scrolling through their phone at the dinner table, while their portal to the outside world lay forbidden on their bedside table.

Screen time is a tool when we change our perspective on it. Not only is it a vital part of modern life but it is also where most of the world's conversation and interaction takes place. As terrifying as this sounds, it is just the way things are. Locking the door on this while our kids' friends play on the other side can be counterproductive in their social lives.

When we lay down these rules from an early age, doing so in a calm and informative manner, our kids will grow up to see technology as the powerful tool that it is. There will of course be days when the sole purpose they use it for will be mindless gameplay, but we need to allow these too or else the active aspects of it will become like a chore to them. Remember, we do not want our kids to hate technology; they must embrace it but only for the right reasons. And sometimes to shoot bad guys, of course.

BEING A GOOD PARENT IS EASIER THAN YOU THINK

Believe us when we say this: You are a good parent. In having gone to the effort to purchase a book about improving your child's well-being, you have proved beyond a doubt that you are caring, loving, worried, intrigued, loyal, and all of the other things that make a wonderful parent. Let's face it: It is a lot easier to just give in and let our kids spend every waking minute online, but you haven't—you are trying to better them and yourself, and that is extremely commendable.

Give yourself a little bit of a break. There is nothing wrong with wanting the best for your kids, and a lot of what we have discussed throughout this book can apply to us, too. Who here does not feel that they spend a little too much time endlessly scrolling? The pitfalls that hide in the undergrowth for our children are there for us, as well—they only look a little different once we fall into them.

A lot of what can affect us online comes from social media. Seeing the polished and *Photoshopped* pictures of our friends' families can make us feel bad when we look down at little Johnny sitting on the floor with Nutella smeared all over his face. However, if we could look behind the camera, we would know that real life happened there, too. They say that a picture is worth a thousand words, but sometimes, the words we want to scream upon seeing these posed images are not suitable for a kiddo's ears.

People lie about their kids or at least exaggerate—we all do it. There is nothing malicious involved, it is just our protective nature used to sugarcoat their achievements from time to time. We just have to know that when someone tells you that their little boy scored four goals in his soccer match, he most probably scored two, and one of them hit his face and went in without him even knowing about it. When they smile proudly and explain that their precious little girl came second in her dance recital, know that only two kids showed up.

This is not to be cruel; it is just to show that too much social media or listening to other parents speak can leave us feeling like we have slipped up somewhere down the road because little Olivia isn't head cheerleader at six.

All of this applies to screen time for our kids. However, much time your friends are saying that their children spent online, add at least another half hour. We all compute it differently in our heads, as a need to convince ourselves that it isn't as bad as we feared kicks in. Yet, it really isn't that bad, and if they spent a little longer gaming last Tuesday when it was raining, then who cares? You got to lie on their bed and watch them enjoying themselves that day, and it was beautiful.

Most of the arguments about the negative side of screen time stem from fear. We are always going to be scared of something that we do not fully understand, and when the perceived effects are not tangible—like a broken bone from skateboarding—it can be a lot harder for us to relax. However, we must let go of some of it. It does not make you a bad parent to want your kid to enjoy themselves, and it certainly does not make you a bad parent to want to make sure that what they are doing isn't hurting them in some way.

Screen time can be a powerful tool for motivation, but we need to try to avoid using it in a threatening way. Positively rewarding our kids with extra screen time is a much healthier approach than negatively threatening bans if certain standards aren't met. The latter will only result in a butting of heads and conflict. Our kids need to know that there are rules in place but also that their opinion and happiness matters.

Of course there are exceptions to any rule and if you have ever road-tripped for an extended period of time then you will know that screens are a way for parents to stay sane. We would all like to think that our pre-teen would just enjoy sitting in the back of a packed vehicle for hours on end, listening to music from their parent's generation while pondering philosophical thoughts as trees pass by…but surprisingly kids don't like that.

Maybe a child in the back with siblings or friends can keep busy for a short time but generally the use of some sort of device will keep the peace. The screen is todays Walkman and Gameboy in one more powerful, smaller unit. Looking in the rear view it may look as though our child is just staring endlessly at their screen but they may just be looking through various music to pick what is next, similar to us rifling through our CD case.

Younger kids that can't ponder the bigger questions in life will just get bored sitting back there. The boredom turns to restlessness which escalates. In this case do not feel guilty about handing them a tablet so you can make the last hour or two of your trip. The screen time rules do not apply in some cases and it is OK to let them slip to help you get to your destination.

Wherever the road trip takes you keep in mind that various ages like various activities. You can assume your pre-teen doesn't want to hang out with adults at your second cousins place or run around and play at a toddler's water park, the same way that your toddler won't be entertained for hours on end at a skate park. As parents we have the duty of "enjoying" both scenarios but if we have to drag the kids around to numerous places then keeping one happy with a screen can buy the other one time to enjoy themselves. Or giving them both a screen can allow you some adult time with your cousins. Overall, this screen time sacrifice will be for the greater good!

Our kids will be into some things that we find strange to us. Their hobbies and interests are what makes them an individual, and when you show a genuine interest in them, you will not only make them immensely happy, you may also find that the thing that was so alien to you is actually a fantastic opportunity for you to bond. You may even end up loving whatever it is just as much as them.

The next time that you are having a bad day and you feel like every decision you make concerning your kids has been wrong, try not to second-guess yourself. The job you are doing is amazing, and the bonds you are building will last forever. When they tell you that, "You are SO not cool," and the bedroom door slams behind them, try to remember that they really will thank you when they're older.

TIME VS. CONTENT

The American Academy of Pediatricians (AAP) recommends around two hours of screen time for kids between two and five. This seems massively high at first glance, but in a world where there is always some form of screen in play, it is actually pretty low. What our kids do during this time is where the problems lie.

Here are some things we can do to find a balance:

- Try using apps that stimulate their creativity.
- Set times during the day when technology is a no-no, with the adults included.
- Find fun activities such as board games or reading to ease out of the transition.
- Insist on the charging of phone and tablets at night to be done in a separate room to your children.
- Cut down on background TV.

- Understand the content that your children are playing or watching.
- Teach them that what they see is not real.
- Understand that it is part of their lives.

Time versus content is an argument that rages internally on the side of screen time. It is a whole other thing to screen time versus no screen time, where the line is firmly drawn in the sand. Problems arise because although both sides agree that screen time is okay when used in moderation, they are unsure of how long should be spent and what should be consumed.

It is just one of a million other issues when we try to break down the positives and negatives, but like so many of them, the answer is a lot clearer than it first appears. All that has happened is that the information has been covered in the spittle of a billion different parents' frantic opinions. Wipe it off and write down one single opinion—yours. Essentially, that is all that matters.

Sure, we have to listen to other people, but only for a moment. At the end of the day, the only decision is ours. The problem with getting caught in the crossfire of everyone speaking at once is that the information gets thrown at you from all different directions. When we take the time to read some facts in a calm and collective way, we can shut off from the incessant voices and notifications on our phone, and make an educated, informed choice.

It is a choice—not just in terms of how long our kids spend on screens, but the content in which they are spending that time. Often, the first half hour that our child is online is spent sorting out who else is on, setting up a game, and getting started. When we come bustling in bang on the hour tapping our watch, they have quite literally only started playing, so their incredulous expression is in some way justified.

We need to try our best to separate the real, intense time spent on screens, with the basic setup or checking of messages. What we consider to be an online activity is sometimes nothing more than a reply to a WhatsApp message or an email. This really should not be considered screen time at all, and unless they use it as a window to start mindlessly scrolling after they have replied, then it is only our kids staying in touch, and we all know that not replying to someone is rude, even if they only typed, "No? Shut up!"

In an article by Jordan Shapiro, a professor at Temple University, concerning our kids and screen time, we are told that we must "integrate devices into their lives in positive ways." This, of course, we have discussed, and it basically boils down to what we already know: Technology in our children's lives is an unavoidable fact. We must learn to point them in the direction of its positive aspects when we can. It can be such a useful tool when used correctly (Quora, 2019).

They add that instead of "micromanaging" their time with screens, we should teach them how to manage it themselves.

Not only in the choices in the content, but in the time spent using technology. When given responsibility, our children can be a lot more mature than we sometimes give them credit for.

Shapiro finishes the article by reassuring us that kids will be kids, and some of the content and time they choose will of course be wrong. However, like everything in a child's progress, we need to nudge them in the right direction and pass down the wisdom that we possess on the matter. We all learn from our mistakes, and the struggles of balancing screen time with face-to-face interaction are just a few more things that they will learn along the way (Quora, 2019).

Everything that we have discussed can become nothing but a pleasant memory when your child's screen time passes over from something that you were moderately worried about to a full-on addiction.

This is a real and serious issue, and it must be viewed as such. Like all addictions, it will take different periods of time to develop in each individual, but unlike many other addictions, kids have easy access to technology. The addictions that we can face as adults—cigarettes, alcohol, or prescription drugs—are all things that we generally don't get introduced to until we are older. Our minds have developed, and we have seen a bit of the world; the choice that we make to first try and then indulge in these things is a little more our own.

Kids these days are born into technology. It is part of their life from the first moment that we hand them a phone in their highchair when they are upset. This again does not make any of us a bad parent, the fact that the age now is a technological one is as far from our doing as it is our kids', but it doesn't take away from the fact that we must be careful when it comes to addiction.

By this we mean, sticking as firmly as you can to regulations. You will not need to set up watchtowers and do hourly marches around the house with a flashlight and a German Shepherd, but you will have to limit the "free days" that we all have to allow. When we are giving our child a treat by letting them have a day where they do nothing but play online, we are doing something quite nice for them. However, when a "treat" becomes an everyday occurrence, then it ceases being a treat at all, and it becomes the norm.

When addiction becomes a real problem, then professional help is the only answer. Do not be ashamed to ask for help and hiding the problem away so your friends do not see and judge you, will be devastating to your child's long-term health. They will need to speak with a medical professional, and suddenly confiscating every tablet, phone, and console in the house will not necessarily solve the problem, as the addiction has already manifested in them.

Again, if this is the case, try not to be overly hard on yourself. You may have dropped the ball a little, sure, but addiction has many different levels of receptiveness in each individual, and the speed and intensity of it can be triggered almost instantly in some. A kid that is born with an addictive personality will most likely be triggered from the moment they first enjoy an online game or the escapism of YouTube. Regardless of the causes, please make the call, and do not be hard on them or yourself if you do.

Finding the balance of time and content can result in a range of emotions and conflicts, from screaming matches to a chirpy nod of agreement. We just hope that when you tell little Johnny and Olivia to switch *Fortnite* to *Wordscapes*, that it is the latter.

CONCLUSION

So, here we are. We hope that some of the topics that have been discussed in this book have not only helped you and your children in laying down some healthier screen time rules but have also provided reassurance and a slightly better perspective on the true positives attached to it.

There are good and bad sides—this we know. Sure, we have tried here to accentuate the sometimes-overlooked wins that we can all take from our child's screen time, but we have always tried to place them fairly beside the losses that we must accept, too.

The biggest and most detrimental of these is, of course, cyberbullying. We think it is fair to say that the idea of some little punk from our child's class sending them abusive messages on their iPhone or Xbox is possibly one of the most painful thoughts that can creep into our heads. When we think of online bullying, especially when directed at our little one, our heart not only breaks a little, it fully shatters and only leaves tiny shards on the ground.

Long gone are the days of a bullied child getting a little reprieve from their torture when the bell goes off at three o'clock, and they can go home and get lost in a comic book, the old black and white TV, or Rock 'n' Roll records, and forget about their tormentors until the following morning. Bullying is a 24-hour experience now, as their chat on Facebook or their feed on Twitter is just another avenue for the kids at school to spread their hate.

Now, we could go into the psychological reasons behind why the kids that are bullying are doing it—their upbringing, their insecurities, or "our child is smarter"—but when your kid is on the end of this torment, none of that is rational to us, and rightly so. All we know is that our little one is being targeted and that they are miserable.

Yet, with the added avenues for bullying to occur, come more options for your kids to feel safe. As we briefly touched on in the section, "Screen Time for Children with Autism and Special Needs," many forums exist for kids who are suffering online abuse to touch base with others who are going through the same thing. Like a lot of issues with younger people, they sometimes do not feel comfortable discussing them with their parents or any adults for that matter. Having an online space where they can share their pain and struggles will not only help them in building up defenses but in creating bonds with others in the same boat.

For our part, we must always be there for our kids when online bullying takes place. By this, we mean we have to be even more understanding where screen time is concerned because if they have found a place that gives them even a moment's escape from the world that they feel has been so cruel to them, then we have to reevaluate our technology limits. Of course, we can also not allow it to become a constant, since running away from our problems in any walk of life is detrimental in the long run, as we all know.

Allowing them into a chat room or a cyberbullying forum will be therapeutic in helping them in understanding that they are not alone. As is the case with most major problems in anyone's life, the feeling that no one else has ever gone through the same thing and that there must be no cure or end to it is always what leads to a feeling of total despair. Letting them be in the company, albeit online, of fellow victims, will be of great comfort to them.

There are several resources for the prevention of bullying and coping with it, and they are of great help to parents of the children and the children themselves. Here is a list of some of the best:

- PACER's National Bullying Prevention Center
- The American Federation of Teachers
- National Runaway Safe line
- National Education Association
- The Bully Project
- Bully Bust
- Safekids.com
- Stop Bullying
- Stomp Out Bullying

If you feel that your child is suffering from online abuse, then you must get proactive and help them to fight back. Contacting one of these wonderful organizations will be a massive first step.

OVERVIEW REVIEW

We cannot finish our time together without discussing why we are here in the first place and what we have learned together. Our kids are the most important things in our life, that is just how it is. When we think of them, we get a feeling of love that cannot be equaled, and the thought that a choice we have made affecting their lives is one of the most painful experiences a parent can have.

However, some decisions will cause damage, and it is unavoidable. What we have tried to do here is to take away some of the stigma attached to one of the perceived worst ones. Screen time will always be a hot topic, or at least until holograms and virtual reality or something else takes over, but for us, right here right now, it is an issue that definitely needs to be addressed. As we think back over everything that we have discussed here, we will keep landing on things that we either knew but were misinformed about, or we now realize actually have a lot of positives that we never considered.

Some of the main takeaways have been that screen time is inevitable. This was always in the background of everything we talked about because it is unavoidable. When we accept it, then the rest of what we learned can begin to be applied. Oftentimes, the thing that we fear the most can be our saving grace. This is not to say that screens are just what our kiddo always needed, so let's plonk them in front of it for hours on end. It is only referring to some of the major strong points that we can edge them toward.

Johnny may love playing *Fortnite* from time to time, but if we intersperse his screen time with an educational game here and there, then he will only reap the benefits. Olivia may like nothing more than to enjoy watching L.O.L. Surprise! toys being unwrapped on YouTube, but if we show her another video where they encourage dancing or learning, then it is "all good in the hood," as the kids used to say.

Raising our kids, and raising them well, is as much about the things that we let them do as it is the things that we don't. Another serious point that runs through this book is that denying our children their time online with their friends can have hugely detrimental effects such as alienation, loneliness, anxiety, and a feeling of being left behind. These emotions can creep over into other aspects of their lives such as study as their general happiness and peace of mind starts suffering. Remember, that *ping* notification when they fire up their console is just the doorbell ringing.

Of course try to get them outdoors, too. We have mentioned the importance of a healthy diet and exercise in our "Cookie Jar" section, and it is always going to be of vital importance. We all know how hard it can be to motivate ourselves to get out and go for a jog or hit the gym for an hour, so for a child whose metabolism has them believing that 15 Big Mac burgers has no effect on them, it can take a little more of a push from our end. Yet, for the younger kids, getting them out will be a lot easier, as more often than not, outdoor activities would be their preference. We just need to pique their interest a little.

Video games and on-screen violence will always be there, and much like technology as a whole, it is in our teaching of right from wrong that will point them in the right direction. Trying to hide them from it completely will be an impossible task, so the best we can do is shield them for as long as possible and prepare them for their inevitable exposure to it. Having them ready and educated on it will help when the time comes.

Remember to lead by example. If no phones during family time is a rule for the kids, then it must be a rule for us. Children pick up on a lot more than we sometimes give them credit for, so we must always be aware that if we tell them that something they are doing is not allowed as we keep one eye on a screen ourselves, then they are naturally going to feel resentment.

For the younger ones, this can be a little harder to explain, as our teens will be more likely to understand when it is work related or an important email. Either way, when there are times that we have laid down the law concerning their usage at the dinner table, then we must to adhere to the stone tablet that we have read to them from. One rule for us and another rule for them is important, sure, but if it only involves us putting the screen down for an hour, then surely we can manage that, right?

One of the most important things of all is always going to be dismissing the opinions of anyone else that you do not respect. When we had this section in the book, it was mentioned early for a reason. We need you to know that what others think about how you are raising your child or the amount of screen time that is being allowed, is much like the acting career of Nicolas Cage, mostly trash with some good stuff sprinkled in here and there. You need to dismiss them as quickly as you can, as letting these poisonous opinions and the people that have them into your reflection will only make an already confusing situation, like screen time, all the harder to navigate.

Remember that your view on the subject is all that matters, and when it comes to something like your children's well-being, then letting in any distractions, especially those of people that you do not respect or even like, will only cause a storm where you don't need one. Through reading this book, you will now be able to make a much more informed decision on how much time and what content your kids watch. However, it will be *your* decision, and that is the most important thing.

There are times in life when we look back at some of the things that caused us pain or worry in the past. Oftentimes, the very issue that had plagued our every waking minute turned out to be nothing to worry about. Now, we are not going to sit here and say that our children's screen time is nothing to be concerned about—that would be silly—but we are trying to convey that it is not always the horrific thing that we are sometimes led to believe. It can even be an extreme positive when harnessed correctly and used as a tool.

One of the more scrutinized ways of using it as a tool is the good old bribe. Ever since the original little Johnny and Olivia started pulling on their parents' loincloths and kicking up a fuss as their parents were trying to go hunting or spring-clean the cave, parents have been using bribery to get their kids to do what they want. It can be a slippery slope when it becomes an everyday occurrence, as our kids will quickly learn that even when they are not upset, a quick, well-acted tantrum will soon get them what they want.

However, slipping them the odd brown envelope with extra wads of screen time in it from time to time will do absolutely no harm if we are in the middle of a good book or *Friends* is on again. Try not to feel guilty for doing this when the opportunity arises. Just be careful that they do not see it so often that they begin taking acting classes on the side.

NOW THAT YOU HAVE THE TOOLS . . .

Now that you have the tools needed to make your decisions on screen time, you can begin to build the technological haven that you have always dreamed of. Rules are there to be broken, of course, and it will always happen, but hopefully, through everything that you have learned in this book, you can put them in place in a way that suits everyone. This will help in the number of times that your children feel the need to chance their arm at sneaking extra screen time, and when they do, you can maybe go a little easier on them with the knowledge that the screen is not the evil you were led to believe it was.

Try and take what we have discussed here and apply it to your child's technology consumption where possible. We all have different circumstances, of course, and we have covered an awful lot of them here, but you will now have more of a big picture of yours and how the information can be applied to your little ones. The trick is to lay down your new conditions and stick to them because when you do, the improvement will be almost magical.

When our kids appreciate technology for what it really is, then their escape time into games and videos will mean a lot more to them—and us. Sharing in our children's joy is a beautiful thing, and when we allow ourselves to relax in the knowledge that they are doing themselves no harm, this becomes a much more enjoyable experience.

They will instinctively know when they have played too long once the teachings that you impart begin to manifest in them. It may take a little time, and there will definitely be arguments and huffs along the way, but that goes for anything worth having in life. The secret is to not let it ruin your day; when it is all said and done, they will become amazing people because of the fantastic parents around them, and a run through the city in *GTA* will never change that.

Try not to be too hard on yourself, and remember to take some time to yourself when you can. We promise you that the repetitive noises from the screen will sound a lot less like a drill if you managed to have lunch with your friends that day. A calmer, more fulfilled parent makes for a calmer and happier household —and a happy household is why we are here now.

Joy in life is where you find it, and sometimes, the places our kids find it is on YouTube. How they watch it and the levels that we know to be detrimental is up to us to impart. This will now come a lot easier to you, and we hope that the next time that you tell them to switch it off does not result in a roll of the eyes.

No matter how many times they tell us that we "just don't get it" or that we're "not cool," we know deep down inside that what we are asking them to do really is for their own good. And hey, we know full well that we are the coolest.

REVIEWS

With an array of self-help books, especially on the subjects of parenting and technology, we need reviews to help us to climb up the commercial ladder, so to speak!

If you enjoyed reading The Guilty Parents—Screen Kids or feel that it has helped you in the battle with screen time, please leave us a review on Amazon. It would be greatly appreciated, and it would help us in our own journey of helping parents along the way.

For more information go to www.TheGuiltyParents.com.
Thank you.

REFERENCES

America's Army. (2019). "America's Army." *Americasarmy.com.* https://www.americasarmy.com/

Anderson, M., & Jiang, J. (2018, Nov 8). *2.* "Teens, friendships and online groups." *Pew Research Center: Internet, Science & Tech; Pew Research Center: Internet, Science & Tech.* https://www.pewresearch.org/internet/2018/11/28/teens-friendships-and-online-groups/

Apple. (ret. 2021, June 5). "Set up Screen Time for a family member on iPad." *Apple Support.* https://support.apple.com/en-ca/guide/ipad/ipadb15cb886/ipados

Ashley, D (2018, July 14). "Teach Your Kids To Manage Their Own Screen Time." *Nurture and Thrive.* https://nurtureandthriveblog.com/screen-time-limits-for-kids/

Barrow, L., Markman, L., & Rouse, C. E. (2007, Oct 28). "Technology's Edge: The Educational Benefits of Computer-Aided Instruction." *SSRN Electronic Journal.* https://doi.org/10.2139/ssrn.1083781

Bellerose, S. (2020, April 30). "Best Youtube Exercise & Fitness Workout Channels for School Aged Kids." *Danceparent101.com.* https://danceparent101.com/best-youtube-exercise-fitness-workout-channels-for-school-aged-kids/

Bennet, D. T. (2021, Feb 3). "Internet Safety for Kids & Teens." *GetKidsInternetSafe.* https://getkidsinternetsafe.com/

Bevalier, D. (2012, June 6). "Your brain on video games." *YouTube.* https://www.youtube.com/results?search_query=Your+brain+on+video+games+%7C+Daphne+Bavelier

Boffey, P. (2019, Nov 1). *Do Violent Video Games Lead to...* Dana Foundation; Dana Foundation. https://dana.org/article/do-violent-video-games-lead-to-violence/

Brandon Carte. (2020, Mar 25). "Work Up a Sweat at Home With These Fitness Video Games." *Best Products.* https://www.bestproducts.com/tech/software/g31708866/fitness-video-games/

Care.com. (2015, Feb 10). "101 indoor games and activities for kids." *Care.com.* https://www.care.com/c/stories/3775/101-indoor-games-and-activities-for-kids/

Casares, W. (2020, July 29). "Importance of Self-Care: Why Parents Need Time Out to Recharge." *HealthyChildren.org.* https://www.healthychildren.org/English/family-life/family-dynamics/Pages/Importance-of-Self-Care.aspx

DeWitt, S. (2017, Oct 19). "3 fears about screen time for kids -- and why they're not true." *YouTube* Www.youtube.com. https://www.youtube.com/watch?v=8woKcr7u-YQ

Dunkley MD, V. L. (2016, Dec 31). "Autism and Screen Time: Special Brains, Special Risks | Psychology Today Canada." *Www.psychologytoday.com.* https://www.psychologytoday.com/ca/blog/mental-wealth/201612/autism-and-screen-time-special-brains-special-risks#:~:text=Individuals%20with%20autism%20are%20typically

Editors of Merriam-Webster. (2019, February 28). A History of Banned Dance Crazes from the Past. The Merriam-Webster.Com Dictionary. https://www.merriam-webster.com/words-at-play/your-grandparents-dirty-dancing-banned-dances-from-history

Engel, L. (2016, Aug 26). "Why The Netflix Of Fitness Just Added A New Platform For Kids." *Forbes.* https://www.forbes.com/sites/lizengel/2020/01/28/whats-next-for-neou-the-netflix-of-fitness-releases-new-classes-for-families/?sh=6420456014db

Erin. (2020, april 19). "5 Apps to Help Kids Stay Connected to Friends and Family." *Stateline Kids.* https://statelinekids.com/

2020/04/19/5-apps-to-help-kids-stay-connected-to-friends-and-family/

Feng, J., & Spence, I. (2008). "How Video Games Benefit Your Brain." *Semantic Scholar.* https://meaningfulplay.msu.edu/proceedings2008/mp2008_paper_76.pdf

Frost, A. (2020, Mar 31). "What Is Mom Guilt? Why Being Gentle With Yourself Matters." *Healthline.* https://www.healthline.com/health/parenting/mom-guilt#effects

Funtech. (2020, Mar 16). "Does Minecraft Make You Smarter: Is it Good for Your Brain / IQ?" *FunTech Blog.* https://funtech.co.uk/latest/does-minecraft-make-you-smarter

Gibbs Venlow, B. (2017, May 10). "No, Moms: It's Not Selfish to Make Yourself a Priority." *Parents.* https://www.parents.com/parenting/moms/healthy-mom/self-care-for-moms-why-its-important-to-make-it-a-priority/

Hiniker, A., Schoenebeck, S. Y., & Kientz, J. A. (2016, May 26). "Not at the Dinner Table: Parents- and Children-s Perspectives on Family Technology Rules." *Proceedings of the 19th ACM Conference on Computer-Supported Cooperative Work & Social Computing - CSCW '16.* https://doi.org/10.1145/2818048.2819940

Hogenboom, M. (2020, Sept 28). "Why not all screen time is the same for children." *Www.bbc.com.* https://www.bbc.com/

future/article/20200925-how-screen-time-affects-childrens-brains

Inc, C. com. (2013, Sept 9). "10 Ways Single Parents Can Get Alone Time." *Care.com*. https://www.care.com/c/stories/5306/how-single-parents-can-get-alone-time/

Jargon, J. (2021, Feb 6). "Violent Videogames Aren't Ruining Your Kids—but It's Good to Discuss Them." *Wall Street Journal*. https://www.wsj.com/articles/violent-videogames-arent-ruining-your-kidsbut-its-good-to-discuss-them-11612620001

Kidslox. (2018, Feb 12). "Active screen time vs passive: a parents guide to healthy screen use." *Kidslox - Parental Controls App for IOS & Android.* https://kidslox.com/blog/active-screen-time-vs-passive/

Kouremetis, D. (2017, Feb 17). "The Gift That Keeps on Giving: Coping with Parental Guilt | Psychology Today Canada." *Www.psychologytoday.com.* https://www.psychologytoday.com/ca/blog/the-unedited-offspring/201702/the-gift-keeps-giving-coping-parental-guilt

Kühn, S., Gleich, T., Lorenz, R. C., Lindenberger, U., & Gallinat, J. (Oct 29, 2013). "Playing Super Mario induces structural brain plasticity: gray matter changes resulting from training with a commercial video game." *Molecular Psychiatry, 19*(2), 265–271. https://doi.org/10.1038/mp.2013.120

Lehman, J. (2021, Jan 12). "Am I a Bad Parent? How to Let Go of Parenting Guilt." *Empowering Parents.* https://www. empoweringparents.com/article/am-i-a-bad-parent-how-to-let-go-of-parenting-guilt/

Lenhart, A. (2015, Aug 6). "Chapter 3: Video Games Are Key Elements in Friendships for Many Boys." *Pew Research Center: Internet, Science & Tech; Pew Research Center: Internet, Science & Tech.* https://www.pewresearch.org/internet/2015/ 08/06/chapter-3-video-games-are-key-elements-in-friendships-for-many-boys/

Lufkin, B. (2020, Dec 16). "How online gaming has become a social lifeline." *Www.bbc.com.* https://www.bbc.com/worklife/ article/20201215-how-online-gaming-has-become-a-social-lifeline

Mack, E. (2019, Oct 22). "Screen Time May Actually Be Good For Kids, New Oxford Study Finds." *Forbes.* https://www. forbes.com/sites/ericmack/2019/10/22/oxford-study-challenges-what-youve-been-told-about-screen-time-and-kids-for-years/?sh=425619a613bd

Mayo Clinic. (2019, June 20). "Tips to manage kids' screen time." *Mayo Clinic.* https://www.mayoclinic.org/healthy-lifestyle/childrens-health/in-depth/screen-time/art-20047952#:~:text=Prioritize%20unplugged%2C%20unstructured%20playtime.

Mccarthy, B., Tiu, M., & Linlin Li. (2014, Sept). "Learning Math with Curious George: PBS KIDS Transmedia and Digital Learning Games in the Preschool Classroom A Report to the CPB-PBS Ready To Learn Initiative." *WestEd.org* https://www.wested.org/wp-content/uploads/2016/11/1456767519resourcelearningmathwithcuriousgeorge-3.pdf

McCarthy, C. (2016, Aug 26). "Protecting children from the dangers of "virtual violence" - Harvard Health Blog." *Harvard Health Blog.* https://www.health.harvard.edu/newsletter_article/violent-video-games-and-young-people

McGonigal, J. (2010, Mar 17). "Gaming can make a better world | Jane McGonigal." *YouTube.* https://www.youtube.com/watch?v=dE1DuBesGYM

Microsoft. (Ret. 2021, June 5). "Set screen time limits on your kids' devices." *Support.microsoft.com.* https://support.microsoft.com/en-us/account-billing/set-screen-time-limits-on-your-kids-devices-a593d725-fc4c-044c-284d-32eab0305ffd

Mom, D. S.-F. (2016, Dec 20). "How to Introduce Screens as an Educational Tool | screenfreeparenting.com." *Screenparenting.com.* https://www.screenfreeparenting.com/introduce-screens-educational-tool/

Morin, K. (2016, Aug 26). "Too Much of a Good Thing? Foods That Can Be Toxic If You Eat Them in Excess." *PartSelect.com.* https://www.fix.com/blog/foods-that-can-be-toxic/

Ortutay, B. (2018, Sept 4). "Before parental "screen time" concerns: radio, even novels." *AP NEWS*. https://apnews.com/article/10a38154c6204b8483ae065605bf929e

Pappas, S. (2020, April 1). "What do we really know about kids and screens?" *Https://Www.apa.org.* https://www.apa.org/monitor/2020/04/cover-kids-screens

Peake, J. (2018, Oct 23). "Screen time for children on the autism spectrum - Altogether Autism." *Altogether Autism.* https://www.altogetherautism.org.nz/screen-time-for-children-on-the-autism-spectrum/

Quora. (2019, Jan 23). "What You Really Need To Know About Screen Time And Your Kids." *Forbes.* https://www.forbes.com/sites/quora/2019/01/23/what-you-really-need-to-know-about-screen-time-and-your-kids/?sh=6d1659c93a0d

Rober, M. (2015, July 2). "How To Come Up With Good Ideas | Mark Rober | TEDxYouth@ColumbiaSC." *YouTube.* https://www.youtube.com/watch?v=L1kbrlZRDvU

Ruder, D. B. (2019, June 19). "Screen Time and the Brain | Harvard Medical School." *Harvard.edu; Harvard Medical School.* https://hms.harvard.edu/news/screen-time-brain

Schmidt, M. E., Pempek, T. A., Kirkorian, H. L., Lund, A. F., & Anderson, D. R. (2008, July 14). "The Effects of Background Television on the Toy Play Behavior of Very Young Children."

Child Development, 79(4), 1137–1151. https://doi.org/10.1111/j.1467-8624.2008.01180.x

Staiano, A. E., & Flynn, R. (2014, Nov 25). "Therapeutic Uses of Active Videogames: A Systematic Review." *Games for Health Journal, 3*(6), *351–365.* https://doi.org/10.1089/g4h.2013.0100

Stillman, J. (2018, Oct 3). "A 70-Year Study of 70,000 Children Says This Is the Secret to Raising Successful Kids." *Inc.com.* https://www.inc.com/jessica-stillman/scientists-followed-thousands-of-kids-for-70-years-this-is-biggest-takeaway-for-parents.html

Sundberg, M. (2018, Feb 19). "Online gaming, loneliness and friendships among adolescents and adults with ASD." *Computers in Human Behavior.* https://doi.org/10.1016/j.chb.2017.10.020

Taylor, M. (2018, Oct 1). "Things to do when Babysitting (206 Kids Games & Activities)." *Kidsit Babysitting Tips.* https://kidsit.com/things-to-do-when-babysitting

Thompson, D. (2018, Sept 27). "Can Too Much Screen Time Dumb Down Your Kid?" *Consumer Health News | Health-Day.* https://consumer.healthday.com/general-health-information-16/media-health-news-760/can-too-much-screen-time-dumb-down-your-kid-738063.html

Yanev, V. (2021, June 22). Video Game Demographics – Who Plays Games in 2021. TechJury. https://techjury.net/blog/video-game-demographics/#gref

Made in United States
North Haven, CT
11 October 2021

10267946R00081